THE
GOSPEL OF LUKE

DBC

INTRODUCING THE

DOUBLEDAY
BIBLE COMMENTARY
SERIES

Congratulations! You are embarking on a voyage of discovery—or redis-
covery. You may feel you know the Bible very well; you may never have
turned its pages before. You may be looking for a fresh way of approaching
daily Bible study; you may be searching for useful insights to share in a
study group or from a pulpit.

The Doubleday Bible Commentary (DBC) series is designed for all
those who want to study the scriptures in a way that will warm the heart as
well as instruct the mind. To help you, the series distills the best of
scholarly insights into the straightforward language and devotional emphasis of a daily Bible guide. Explanations of background material, and discussions of the original Greek and Hebrew, will always aim to be brief.

• If you have never really studied the Bible before, the series offers a
serious yet accessible way in.

• If you help to lead a church study group, or are otherwise involved in
regular preaching and teaching, you can find invaluable "snapshots" of a
Bible passage through the DBC approach.

• If you are a church worker or minister, burned out on the Bible, this
series could help you recover the wonderful world of scripture.

DOUBLEDAY BIBLE COMMENTARY

THE
GOSPEL OF
LUKE

HENRY WANSBROUGH

DOUBLEDAY BIBLE COMMENTARY
DOUBLEDAY
NEW YORK · LONDON · TORONTO · SYDNEY · AUCKLAND

DOUBLEDAY BIBLE COMMENTARY

PUBLISHED BY DOUBLEDAY

a division of Bantam Doubleday Dell Publishing Group, Inc.

1540 Broadway, New York, New York 10036

DBC, DOUBLEDAY, and the portrayal of an anchor with a dolphin are
trademarks of Doubleday, a division of Bantam Doubleday Dell
Publishing Group, Inc.

Library of Congress Cataloging-in-Publication Data

Wansbrough, Henry, 1934–
The Gospel of Luke / Henry Wansbrough. — 1st U.S. ed.
p.   cm.
1. Bible, N.T. Luke—Commentaries.   2. Bible, N.T. Luke—
Devotional literature.   I. Title.
BS2595.3.W36   1998
226.4'07—dc21   98-3804
CIP

ISBN 0-385-49018-6

Contents

THE PROLOGUE

The Good News of Salvation

THERE IS ALWAYS an excitement in starting to read a Gospel. This is the good news of salvation! Even those last four familiar words introduce a couple of concepts that seemed special for Luke, "good news" and "salvation."

The Greek word translated as "good news" was familiar around the Mediterranean world, which was all part of the Roman Empire. The expression was used of special items of good news about the emperor and his family, such as a victory or the birth of an heir. This "good news" was flashed around the world (it took about four days from Rome to Alexandria by ship), and the different communities sent back congratulatory gifts to the emperor. Luke does not use the noun "good news," but only the verb "proclaim the good news." This has a link to the fine passage in Isaiah 61, "He has sent me to bring the news to the afflicted, to soothe the broken-hearted, to proclaim liberty to captives." And indeed Luke is always mindful of Jesus' announcement precisely to such underprivileged people.

The Preface to the Gospel

MANY SHORT SCIENTIFIC treatises have survived from the first century, works on astronomy, medicine, arms manufacture, and navigation, as well as little historical booklets of about the same size as Luke's work. This formal preface—and Luke is the only Gospel to have such a preface—identifies his work as a short scientific monograph. He clearly wants to introduce his two-volume work (the Acts of the Apostles is the second volume) as just such a scientific historical treatise.

Both volumes are addressed to Theophilus, with the complimentary title "your Excellency" which suggests that he was a high-ranking official. This again adds dignity to the work, though we can never know whether Theophilus was a real person. His name means "friend of God." Whether he was a real person or not, the name suggests the attitude needed for reading the Gospel. It is no use reading the Gospel as simply a scientific or historical work. It must be approached with prayer and openness to God, a willingness to listen to a friend, to accept the message and respond to it.

Luke the Historian

LUKE STRESSES THAT the teaching he conveys is "well-founded" or "safe." He has checked it carefully with eyewitnesses and ministers of the word. He does not want to leave his readers in any doubt about the reliability of his message. Yet there are ways in which his Gospel differs from the Gospels of Mark and Matthew, which came before him. What about these differences? When the evangelists differ from one another, is one right and the other wrong?

Luke certainly rearranges his material to make it an attractive and well-told story. Matthew collected together much of the teaching of Jesus and presents it as the Sermon on the Mount; Jesus is teaching on a mountain, as Moses did, giving his new law as Moses gave the old Law. Luke has a similar collection, but it is a Sermon on the Plain, and much shorter, as though Luke thought there was too much to digest at one sitting. Some of the same sayings of Jesus are placed by Luke in Jesus' great final journey to Jerusalem. Jesus is going up to Jerusalem to die—as all prophets must die at Jerusalem—and gives much of his most important teaching in the course of that journey.

The Sermon anyway occurs later in Luke. Instead, Luke puts early in Jesus' ministry the incident when Jesus' own townsfolk try to throw him off the cliff. It looks in Mark and Matthew as though this incident happened later, after the call of the first disciples. But Luke brings it in at the beginning and makes it the occasion when Jesus gives his important opening proclamation, "The Spirit of the Lord is on me," and he will bring healing not to his own compatriots but to the Gentiles beyond the frontiers of his people.

PRAYER

Open my eyes and ears, Lord, to your good news of salvation.
Help me to listen to your historian, Luke, as he tells the story of how you save the world through your Son, Jesus Christ.

ZECHARIAH AND ELIZABETH

LUKE'S STORY BEGINS in Jerusalem, in the temple, and this is no accident. We are being told that God's promises were first and foremost to Israel, and that they were fulfilled in Jesus. So the story starts in an atmosphere of the best piety of the Old Testament. Zechariah was a priest, and his wife, too, was of the line of Aaron; so they both belonged to the most sacred part of the sacred people. Both, also, were "upright in the sight of God," observing the Law in all its details.

The Law was no tiresome, restricting force, but a liberating, joyful gift. "Your Law, O God, is my life," cries the psalmist so often; "Your Law is a light to my eyes." Its detailed prescriptions helped to bring every moment of life into conscious association with the Lord. I remember an Israeli Jew picking me a banana from a tree in the Plain of Sharon. Before he ate his own banana, he blessed God for it, and explained to me the joy of thanking God for even such a little gift. The Law was the proof of God's special love for Israel, God's special closeness to his people that he should want their life to accord with his, their life to be lived according to his principles. It was also the Law that made sure that every individual was kept free to serve God, could stand tall and proud before God, dependent only on God rather than on any human master.

The Temple of Jerusalem

JERUSALEM PLAYS AN important part in Luke's story. The Gospel begins and ends there. The second half of the Gospel consists of Jesus' great journey to Jerusalem, where he takes possession of the temple and uses it as his own platform for his teaching. It is at Jerusalem that the great events of the Passion are played out, and in Luke's account Jesus appears after his resurrection in and around Jerusalem. The first Christian community, which Luke paints in such inspiring colors in the Acts of the Apostles, is at Jerusalem. It is from Jerusalem that the gospel spreads to the nations.

The center of Jerusalem was the temple. It was this that made Jerusalem, says the Roman author Pliny, "far the most distinguished city of the East." The temple itself was an amazing building, as one can still today guess from the huge esplanade on which it stood, the size of twelve football fields. There were ten gilded gates, each of which was closed every evening (on rollers) by a team of twenty men. The biggest of the great stones which the disciples admired ("Master, look at the size of these stones!") is the size of a modern bus and weighs four hundred tons. Saint Patrick's Cathedral would fit comfortably twice into one of the colonnaded porticoes around the perimeter. It was thronged by Jewish pilgrims who came gratefully from their exile in the Diaspora, especially at the great feasts such as Passover or Pentecost, for this was the place of God's presence on earth, the meeting place between God and his people, gathered from all over the world. One can understand why love for the temple played such a part in every Jewish heart.

Barrenness

DEVOTED TO THE temple and the service of God though they were, this old couple seemed condemned to be childless. God seemed to have neglected their dogged fidelity to him. On every level this was a disaster. No lively family to keep them young. No grandchildren to spoil. No support in old age, in an era when only children could be expected to provide support for the elderly. No hope for the future. And especially for a Jewish couple a full family was (and is) the sign of a special blessing. Most of all in such an age of expectation, no possibility that their child would be the promised Messiah, the hope of every Jewish mother. "Elizabeth was barren and they were both advanced in years." It seemed like the end. No one familiar with the Old Testament could fail to think of Abraham and his wife Sarah, who were nomads without hope in their childless old age when Abraham received the promise of God. So the stage is set for the loving and merciful intervention of God to save his faithful servants.

PRAYER

Lord, you leave me sometimes in a situation where I can see no way out.
Keep me trusting in your love, however dark the horizon. Help me to
know that I am always in your presence, and that you prepare for me
greater blessings that I could ever hope.

THE MESSAGE TO ZECHARIAH

Two Panels

THESE TWO CHAPTERS of the infancy stories are built on a comparison: John the Baptist is compared to Jesus. In each comparison the importance and sanctity of John serves to show the even greater importance and sanctity of Jesus. John and Jesus in these stories look to each other, comparable but with a difference. First we see how John is the climax of all the hopes of the Old Testament, then we see how Jesus is even greater than John.

First there are the two annunciations, to Zechariah and to Mary. In each case, an angel comes to tell that a son will be born against all hope and all natural means. In each case, the birth is an occasion for celebration of those around. In each case, the moment of religious dedication is the occasion for a prophecy of the future greatness and role of the child. The Visitation joins the two panels together.

In each scene, the contrast also goes into detail. Zechariah and Elizabeth are "upright in the sight of God," but Mary "enjoys God's favor." The one child will be called John (most Hebrew names have a meaning, and this means "the grace of God," but the other will be called Jesus, "Savior." John will be "great in the sight of the Lord" and will be dedicated to God as a nazirite ("he must drink no wine, no strong drink"), but Jesus will be called Son of the Most High. John will prepare a people fit for the Lord, but Jesus will rule over the house of Jacob forever. Zechariah doubts the angel's message and loses the power of speech, but Mary believes and receives a blessing.

A Biblical Scene

THE STORY OF this pious couple is the final stage in the process of God preparing a people for himself. The angel's appearance to Zechariah reminds the reader of the appearance of an angel to the mother of Samson in Judges 13. She also was barren when an angel of the Lord Yahweh appeared to her and told her she would conceive and give birth to a son. The son should be dedicated to the Lord, and even while he was in the womb his mother should drink no wine or fermented liquor. The Spirit of God was upon him, too, for his mission.

Abraham also received a similar visit from the angel of Yahweh to promise that his barren wife, Sarah, would bear him Isaac (Genesis 18). The purpose of these stories is not merely to relate miraculous happenings. It is to underline two lessons: first, that God furthers the history of his own people with tireless watchfulness, sending his own Spirit on his chosen leaders. Secondly, God does not rely on human ability, skill, or achievement, but chooses the most unlikely person to be his envoy and further his purposes. In the more ordinary circumstances of our daily lives, one never knows when a dazzling insight or a valuable correction may come from the most unlikely source, which one can afterward see to have been a message from the Lord. In the case of Zechariah and Elizabeth, they were "has-beens," ready to sink into decrepitude and oblivion. Then they received the dazzling mission of rearing John to prepare a people fit for the Lord.

Scenes in a Drama

LUKE IS SUCH a neat artist with words! He tells these stories in the language of the Old Testament, imitating the formulas of the Greek Old Testament ("In the days of X," "It came to pass that," and so on) to remind us that we are witnessing the climax of that long preparation. But also each scene of these two chapters of the infancy stories is neat and well wrapped in itself. Each begins with an entrance ("There appeared to him the angel of the Lord") and concludes with an exit ("And when he came out . . ."). Each scene contains a lively dialogue between the two chief characters to convey the message that is the point of the scene. The contrast with Matthew's infancy stories is marked: there, no human being speaks to any other, Joseph never even explains to Mary why he is dragging her off to Bethlehem or Egypt! Matthew has no memorable characters like Zechariah and Elizabeth or Simeon and Anna.

PRAYER

Lord, grant that I, too, may have some part in preparing the way of the Lord, in making ready a people fit for you. Help me to realize that any work of mine for you is empty unless it is built on my own full dedication to you.

THE ANNUNCIATION TO MARY

IF THE BIBLICAL backcloth to Zechariah's message is the annunciation to Samson's mother, to Mary's annunciation the backcloth is the message to Samuel's mother in I Samuel 1. Hannah seems destined to remain childless, when she receives a message of assurance from Eli the priest that her prayer for a son will be answered. She presents the longed-for child to Eli with a song of joy very similar to Mary's *Magnificat*. But the prophecies about Mary's son take us straight back to the prophecies Nathan made to David: "The Lord God will give him the throne of his ancestor David" forever. He will be Son of the Most High, just as Nathan promised David that his descendants would rule forever, and that God would always treat them with the gentleness of a father.

Mary

WHAT WAS MARY'S reaction to all this? The normal age for a girl's betrothal in those days was soon after the twelfth birthday (for boys four years later). We certainly do not have to think of a scene like a Fra Angelico painting, Mary kneeling piously at a prie-dieu, while a winged and feathered angel addresses her. The angel need not have taken any physical form at all, and no audible word need have been spoken. It was a message from God, and the Gospel—though it delights in visual and imaginable details—is careful to give no physical description of God's messenger. The angels are the powers of God and need no feathers.

I like to imagine this young Galilean girl, intrigued by the budding of her own sexuality, excited at the prospect of marriage, daydreaming while she feeds the family chickens or brings water from the well. At a certain moment she knows that God is calling her (we can use only physical terms, as though she heard a sound!) to bear a son by the power of the Most High. What was that son to be? To a people who knew the Bible, the best way of describing his future greatness is in terms of the promises made to David about the special favor God would show his royal line.

Mary's child would fulfill these promises of a son who would reign forever. God would be a father to him, and he a son to God. How much did Mary understand about her son? It is not necessary to suppose that she already understood his divinity. How much do the words of the dialogue owe to Luke's later understanding and formulation? They certainly accord better with the disciples' understanding and language after the resurrection than with their first puzzled and wondering reactions.

Mary's Consent

THE TWO CLUES to Mary's spirituality as Luke sees it seem to me to come at beginning and end. At the beginning comes the greeting "you who enjoy God's favor." St. Jerome, who translated the Gospels into Latin, read this as "full of grace," which suggests a fluid-filled receptacle, and grace has often been represented as a divine fuel or a current of divine power for good action. Rather, it is the unmerited favor of an all-powerful ruler who needs to justify his deeds to no one; he simply chooses his favorites unpredictably and showers his gifts upon them as he will. Primarily it is the personal relationship, the choice and the love, and only secondarily the gifts, the graces that follow. So God simply fixed his choice upon Mary quite arbitrarily, not for any merits of hers.

At the end comes Mary's reply. "Behold, the handmaid of the Lord" may be rendered in more modern terms, "You see before you the Lord's servant." Absolute consent, without conditions. The meaning may be deeper yet if we see an allusion to Isaiah's Songs of the Servant of the Lord. The four Songs depict a servant who yields absolutely to the Lord's will, to end in suffering and humiliation, before final vindication. Jesus certainly spoke of himself in these terms, and it is attractive to see his mother also using this terminology to signify her utter, unconditional assent to God's call. Amid all the excitement, the young girl will have realized that no great task is easy. Luke shows her pledging in these terms the suffering and endurance that her consent implied. In this, as elsewhere in Luke's Gospel, Mary is the first and most faithful model for her son's disciples.

MARY'S VISIT TO ELIZABETH

Mary's Kindness

THERE ARE SEVERAL dimensions to the story of Mary's visit to Elizabeth. It is the first story in Luke of human kindness and affection, qualities that are so important in this Gospel. It is a week's walk from Nazareth to the territory of Judah, an expedition into a different world, and yet Mary goes to support her aging relative and share with her the excitement and worries of pregnancy. From a literary point of view it is thoroughly satisfying that the two separate annunciations should be so linked before the two separate birth stories. The two panels are here brought together. But there is also a touching appreciation of the human dimension: The delight of the two mothers-to-be in their babies and their concentration on them comes to delightful expression in their conversation. There is something especially charming in the way the older woman bows to the younger and addresses her with a formal, biblical beatitude, "Blessed is she who believed," to which the younger replies with the youthful outpouring of her heart in the *Magnificat*. Luke's writing always has great delicacy, which comes to full expression here.

Fulfillment

THERE IS NEVER any doubt that the process taking place is guided in detail by God's plan. Of this Luke gives us little indications, and especially of prophecies made in the course of the Gospel story and fulfilled later within the story. In the annunciation to Zechariah we had heard of John that "even from his mother's womb he will be filled with the Holy Spirit." To anyone who knows the Bible, this was a hint that he would be a prophet like Jeremiah, whose prophecies begin "The word of Yahweh came to me, saying, " 'Before I formed you in the womb I knew you, before you came to birth I consecrated you.' " Now we see John fulfilling the angel's word, silently prophesying by his movement in the womb. The movement itself is charmingly described: The word used for "leapt" is normally used for a dance of joy or the skipping and gamboling of lambs, and the word translated "joy" indicates thrill, delight, and excitement.

"Mother of My Lord"

ELIZABETH'S GREETING SLIPS out so easily that one can easily miss its import. The title "Lord" has already been used in the infancy stories a dozen times, each time signifying the Lord God, the initiator of the whole chain of events. Now for the first time it is used of Jesus. This one word is an excellent measure of the gradually deepening understanding and appreciation of the person of Jesus during the development of the New Testament. It was the word used in the Greek Bible to translate the unpronounceable Name of God, Yahweh. The Name is full of awe and dignity. In the earliest Gospel (Mark), "Lord" is used of Jesus only by people speaking to Jesus, calling him "Lord!" in which sense it can mean no more than "Sir!" Apart from this, it is used only of the Lord God. Matthew advances on this only at the empty tomb, speaking of "the place where the Lord lay" (28:6, AV). By the time of Luke, faith in the divine status of Christ shines through in the almost careless way in which "Lord" may be used either of the Lord God or of Jesus the Lord: 7:13, "When the Lord saw her he felt sorry for her," etc. Here truly it is the Lord God, walking upon earth. So the import of Elizabeth's greeting to "the mother of my Lord" is staggering.

Now here not only is the baby John "filled with the Spirit from his mother's womb" as Zechariah had already been told, but his mother, too, as she is inspired to bless Mary.

A Spirit-Filled World

LUKE IS CONSTANTLY reminding us that every movement in the advance of the gospel is guided by the Spirit. This is less evident when Luke is following Mark's Gospel (roughly from the baptism of Jesus till the story of the empty tomb), but more when he is writing more freely on his own, in these infancy stories, in the resurrection appearances, and above all in the Acts of the Apostles.

REFLECTION
Of all women you are the most blessed, and blessed is
the fruit of your womb.

THE *MAGNIFICAT*

ONE OF THE most attractive features of Luke's infancy narratives is the three lovely and joyful canticles sung over the two children. A well-known scripture scholar has said, "As soon as Jesus is born, everyone bursts into song." Indeed, it happens even before the birth of Jesus. These songs, Mary's *Magnificat*, Zechariah's *Benedictus*, and Simeon's *Nunc Dimittis*, now taken over into Christian liturgy, express wonderfully the joy and gratitude of the three principal adults in these stories, drawing Christians to share in their feelings. One can imagine the overflowing joy of the young girl at meeting her elderly relative. At last she can fully share on intimate terms the secret and the pent-up feelings of approaching motherhood which she has been cherishing since she gave her consent at the annunciation.

The song of Mary falls obviously into three parts, the first five lines telling of what the Lord has done for Mary herself, the last seven drawing the wider consequences for the world—all these built on verbs of action. They are jointed together at the center by a couplet reflecting on the generosity of God: "Holy is his name, and his faithful love extends age after age to those who fear him."

The Poor of Yahweh

THE SONG ECHOES most closely the song of Hannah at the birth of her son, Samuel. Hannah had been considered barren, and, though loved by her husband, this was the tragedy of her life until the Lord gave her a son, whom she dedicated to the Lord. The similarity with Mary's situation is obvious.

The spirit of the song is, however, more widely applied than to just one individual. Mary expresses the sentiment of all Israel, and in this way, too, is the spearhead of the whole people. Ever since the exodus from Egypt, Israel had relied on God's protection for its very survival. In Egypt the Hebrews had been a depressed, hated, and alien minority. In the desert they had felt themselves utterly dependent on God—and the lonely starkness of the desert is a great place for anyone to experience the presence and power of God. After the settlement in Canaan, the Spirit of God, descending upon the "judges," had rescued his people from repeated foreign dominations. As wealth of the nation increased, so did oppression of the poor and helpless. Accordingly, at the Babylonian Exile, the remnant of the people as a whole saw themselves as the wretched and oppressed, dependent for their existence on the generosity of Yahweh. This became a central theme in their spirituality, and the later prophets and the psalms see God above all as the deliverer of the oppressed.

With the coming of the Romans, and the increasing poverty and oppression that this brought, as well as the domination of many people by very few, a longing for deliverance grew ever stronger and more vocal. So throughout the infancy stories we are made aware of the helplessness of those to whom the Lord sends his salvation. Old Zechariah and Elizabeth are childless. Mary can find no house to give birth. Hireling shepherds are the first to hear the good news. Mary and Joseph can afford only the offering of the very poor.

Mary thanks the Lord for the answer she has received to her own perfect gift of herself to God, and for the response that this implies to the prayers of all those who depend on God. The phrases of her prayer are drawn almost entirely from the grateful pleas of the poor in the prophetic literature. She personifies the remnant of Israel.

Faithful Love

THE THEME OF her song is, in effect, "his faithful love," an expression that comes twice in the hymn, as it does also in Zechariah's song. "For his faithful love endures forever" is the continuous refrain of Psalm 136. Matthew three times repeats the phrase of Hosea, "What I want is faithful love, not sacrifice." So this idea of faithful love is at the very center of Israel's concept of God. It was first proclaimed by God himself in the desert of Sinai as the meaning of his name. It remained in the forefront of Israel's mind, alluded to constantly in the scriptures. God is a God not of anger but of generous and enduring forgiveness. And human beings must show this quality too.

PRAYER

The more helpless I am, Lord, the more I throw myself on your faithful love. Help me to avoid all arrogance, pride, and pomposity. Let me remember that all my hope is in you, O Lord.

THE BIRTH OF JOHN THE BAPTIST

The Birth of a Son

THE STORIES OF these two chapters form two panels, comparing and contrasting the two families, and principally the two boys. The two stories have been linked together at the Visitation, and now they separate again. The overwhelming impression of this first scene of birth is bustle and joy, family and neighbors fussing around to share in Elizabeth's joy at the son she had never expected to bear. The contrasting factor at the birth of Jesus will be joy in heaven: At John's birth the joy is on earth, from the neighbors and relations. At the birth of Jesus the angels in heaven, as well as the shepherds on earth, will rejoice.

What's in a Name?

NAMES ARE ALWAYS significant to the Hebrew mind. It was felt that they somehow constituted the person. So when God brought all the wild animals to Adam and he named them, he was in a way giving them their nature, constituting them as themselves and asserting his Godlike sovereignty over them. There are many stories in the Old Testament that explain the names of characters: "Isaac" in Hebrew means, or is close to meaning, "will smile/laugh" (originally an abbreviation for "God will smile on him") and this element of smiling recurs frequently in the stories: Sarah smiling in the tent, Isaac laughing with Ishmael. "Jacob," more ominously, means "will supplant," which is realized in his supplanting his brother Esau. When Jacob has finally abandoned his trickiness and becomes respectable, God gives him a new name, "Israel," as a sign of approval and adoption. So, later in the Gospel story, Jesus will give a new name to Simon, "Peter," and so create him "Rock" of foundation. (It must surely originally have been a nickname that was soon found to have special significance.)

The name "John" is a combination of the shortened divine name "Yahweh," or "Ja," and the word for "grace" or "favor." So "God will show him favor." This provides one more link between the two families, reminding the reader of the angel's greeting to Mary, "you who enjoy God's favor." The name itself has a certain nationalistic ring to it, ever since the Maccabean leader John, who had led the Jews in the second century. The Maccabees had been the spearhead of resistance to Greek attempts to dissolve the Jews and their religion into the common culture of the eastern Mediterranean. So the name John itself proclaims that Israel is the special object of God's favor, for whom God has a special regard and special plans.

Obedience

LUKE IS CONSTANTLY aware of the importance of obedience to God's commands. Mary is the first disciple and model of disciples by her obedience and acceptance of God's word through the angel. So now Zechariah wins back his voice by insisting on obedience to the angel's choice of a name for his son, flying in the face of family tradition. The angel said he would be John and John he shall be! It is also an example of Luke's constant care to show his reader the fulfillment of prophecies made in the course of the Gospel, reminding the Gospel reader of God's constant guiding hand in this vital moment of history: what he promises he brings to fulfillment.

PRAYER

Lord, the birth of a child is always a sign of your favor,
a pledge of your continuing gift of life, now and hereafter. We thank
you for the children born today, and pray that they may be loved.
May they be guided to recognize and respond to your love. May they
also in their lives show your love to others.

THE *BENEDICTUS*

God's Promises Fulfilled

ZECHARIAH'S JOYFUL SONG of praise falls into two halves, the first looking back to the promises of God which are now fulfilled, the second looking forward to the prophetic role of the child so recently born.

Zechariah (and through him the evangelist) sees these events as the fulfillment and culmination of the whole of the Old Testament. This is clear from the mention of those two central historical figures, David and Abraham. They stand for the two major periods of Israel's history, the time of the patriarchs and the time of the kingdom. Mention of the promises to Abraham immediately brings to mind the promise that his descendants would be as the stars of the sky or the sands on the seashore. Mention of the promises to David brings to mind the promise that David's descendants would inherit a throne forever, and that God would consider them as his sons, correcting them as a parent corrects children. These were the two pillars on which Israel's hope was built during the dark days of the exile and the subsequent oppression of the impoverished and powerless remnant.

Matching these two significant figures are two evocative concepts, the covenant and God's faithful love. The covenant was the basis of Israel's existence. The group of escaped slaves around Moses were at their lowest ebb: They had been oppressed in Egypt and subjected to ethnic cleansing as the hated remnant of a dominating foreign power. Escaping, they were pursued into the wastes of Sinai, where only the most experienced small group can survive, and even complained that they longed to return to the fleshpots, the leeks, and the garlic of Egypt. At this moment God created them a people, and his own people, a people closer to their God than any other people had been; he made with them a covenant, promising them his own protection. This was an agreement, like an alliance between two powers, or an overlord and a subject people. Israel was to be God's people: He would protect them and they would be faithful to him. This was the basis of their life, of their very existence as a people.

And then, when they had so quickly deserted him by worshiping the golden calf (or bull), he proclaimed the meaning of his name as faithful love. The prophet Hosea gave a new intensity to the concept by his imagery of this love as the passionate and unshakable love of a man for his unfaithful wife. Another dimension is the family love of siblings who stand by each other in ultimate distress and disaster. This was the love God showed by bringing his promises to their fulfillment. It is the key to the first part of Zechariah's canticle.

Freedom

GOD HAS VISITED his people and set them free, proclaims Zechariah. Free from oppression or from sin? The domination of the Romans was certainly hated, but just how oppressive it was remains disputed. There was financial and economic distress, and the distress of uncured sickness. But there is no firm evidence that there was widespread dire penury and want. In this canticle it is more likely that Zechariah has in mind primarily the freedom to serve the Lord.

Prophet of the Most High

JOHN IS TO be a prophet preparing the way for the Lord, as will be seen when his ministry begins. He is to proclaim forgiveness and repentance for salvation, paving the way for Jesus' own message of forgiveness. As such, he is the prototype also of the Christian apostle, for the apostles in Acts in the same way are filled with the Spirit. The apostles, too, proclaim forgiveness in their call to repentance at the end of each of their sermons in Acts.

He is to "guide our feet into the way of peace." By so doing he begins the mission that will continue into the mission of the disciples. In Luke, Jesus characteristically brings peace by his miracles. The angels sing "Peace on earth" at Jesus' birth. The crowds proclaim peace in heaven at Jesus' entry into Jerusalem. Missioners are told by Jesus to bring peace where they go, and to Cornelius, Peter describes Jesus' message as the good news of peace. Peace, reconciliation, and forgiveness are the watchwords of Luke's Christian message.

PRAYER

The rising Sun from on high has come to visit us, to give light to those who live in darkness and the shadow dark as death.

THE BIRTH OF JESUS

❧

Luke the Popular Historian

LUKE IS A historian, and is careful to show that Jesus' birth is an event in world history. So he dates the birth of Jesus in relation to the great Roman emperor, Augustus, and the census of tribute. The provinces of the empire paid tribute to Rome, but during much of King Herod's reign, as a dependent sovereign Palestine had been exempt. It was only after Herod invaded a neighbor and excited the emperor's anger that tribute was imposed. The first assessment of resources to be taxed roused great opposition and petty revolts, and was remembered years later. However, Quirinius is now known to have been governor of Syria in A.D. 6–7, and it is also highly unlikely that all the populace would have had to register in the town of their remote ancestors. Luke was not a modern research-historian; he simply uses well-known figures and events of about that time to link his story to world history. We do not know exactly when Jesus was born. For the believer, this ignorance itself has a message as part of Christ's reversal of values: The Son of God was born not in the capital city of an empire but in a tiny hill-village of an obscure country. We do not know his age or his birthday (December 25 was chosen later because it was the pagan feast-day of the rebirth of the sun after the winter solstice). As the people of Jerusalem say in John's Gospel: "When the Christ appears, no one will know where he comes from." In fact, the place is better known than the time: The one firm element about the tradition (in both Matthew and Luke) is that he was a Nazarene, but was born in Bethlehem.

A Poor and Obscure Birth

LUKE GOES OUT of his way to emphasize that Jesus was born in poor circumstances, with none of the advantages of position, despite being of the line of David. His parents were migrants, friendless in the town, and could find no place for the mother to give birth. There was no space for them in the *kataluma*. This Greek word does not mean "inn," as the old

Latin translation goes. So the Christmas images of inhospitable innkeepers have no place in the story. We need to imagine a large, open dwelling room on two levels. The humans are on one level, the animals at a slightly lower level. As the level for the humans is too crowded even for a precious newborn baby, Mary leans over to place her baby in the hay-filled feeding trough of the cattle. And so our Christmas crib scene is completed by the ox and the ass. They are not mentioned in the Gospel, but in Isaiah 1 the devotion of the ox and the ass to their master is contrasted with Israel's infidelity.

In Matthew, Jesus' first recorded visitors are Oriental sages. In Luke, they are simple shepherds. Later rabbinic tradition regarded shepherds as unclean. Though this was not yet in force, night-shift shepherds were surely low on the social scale. But the shepherds also remind us that the child will be the shepherd of Israel.

The Song of the Angels

JESUS MAY BE born the son of a homeless migrant, but his true significance is proclaimed by the angels. There may not be an extended family to rejoice around the newborn (as there was for John), but there is joy in heaven. The canticle is spoken not by Zechariah but by God's own messengers. The good news is announced not just to Zechariah but to the people, to Israel as a whole. The three titles they give to the baby are full of awesome promise. The Christ or Messiah, born in the city of David, is the fulfillment of all human hopes, but "savior" and "lord" are properly divine titles. Previously these had always been applied to God, never to a human being.

The waves of praise, song, and joy succeed one another: the great army of heaven, the shepherds as they bustle along, all those who heard their news, and the shepherds again as they disappear back into the night.

PRAYER

Lord, with your birth as a human child you transformed the world. You became one of us so that you could take us to yourself and give us a share in your divine life. Let me treasure this honor and realize my dignity.

JESUS IN THE TEMPLE

The Faithful of Israel

THE FIRST INCIDENT told after the birth of Jesus stresses the lesson we have already heard, that Jesus is the fulfillment of God's promises, coming to the faithful of Israel. The parents of Jesus fulfill the Law rigorously, first by circumcision, then by the purification—indeed overzealously, for Joseph goes up to fulfill it too, when in fact by the Law only the mother is purified. Still, it is underlined that they are among the poor, for they can afford the offering only of the very poor. According to Leviticus, "If she cannot afford a lamb, she must take two turtledoves or two young pigeons" and offer their life as a symbol of recognition that all life comes from God.

There they are welcomed by the two representatives of Israel, Simeon and Anna. They represent the patient faithful, for their great age and their joy denote their patient waiting. The life of both is centered on the piety of the temple. Simeon is already so full of the Spirit that the Spirit prompts him to come forward at the exact moment. Anna also has spent her life "serving God night and day with fasting and prayer," the two traditional good works of the Law. The fact that the third traditional good work, almsgiving, is omitted shows that she is one of the faithful poor of Yahweh, too poor to exercise this good work. She has no canticle of her own, but as a prophetess spreads the good news of the child "to all who looked forward to the deliverance of Jerusalem." Both of them are full of that lively praise of God, which makes the infancy stories so positive and enthusiastic.

The Canticle of Simeon

WITH SIMEON A new vista opens up. His joyful song welcomes the child as the "glory for your people Israel" but also as "a light of revelation for the Gentiles," the first indication of a theme that will be so important to Luke. Writing for an audience formed in the culture of the Greco-Roman world, he points out again and again that Jesus brings salvation to all nations, not only to Israel. Again the wonderful symbol of light is used.

Zechariah had sung that the child was the rising Sun come from on high to visit us, those who sit in darkness. Now the light spreads to the Gentiles. However, salvation is first for Israel, as Luke has shown us throughout these two chapters. But the first note of sadness creeps in with the hint of rejection. The child is destined for the fall as well as the rise of many in Israel, a sign that will be opposed. Both division and sadness will be the lot of Mary herself, by the piercing of her heart with a sword. Already the shadow of the cross hangs over the tender child and his mother. One may surmise also that the rejection of her son by so many of her own people was itself a sadness to her, a cause of division in her heart.

Sexual Equality

THE MEETING AND prophecy in the temple is the first really clear instance of the careful representation by Luke that men and women have equal value before the Lord, an insistence that runs through his work. Already we have had the two annunciations, to Zechariah and to Mary. Here we have Simeon and Anna. Later, Jesus will point out that the prophet brought salvation to the widow of Zarephath and the man Naaman. Two miracle stories open respectively "There before him was a woman" and "There in front of him was a man" (13:11 and 14:2). Two models of persevering prayer are the friend at midnight and the persevering widow. In other lessons on prayer the contrast between the Pharisee and the tax collector is balanced by the contrast between Martha and Mary.

In the spread of the gospel in Acts, the same equality continues. Ananias and Sapphira are both punished for their sin. Aeneas and Tabitha are both healed in the neighboring towns of Lydda and Joppa. At Athens the man Dionysius and the woman Damaris are both mentioned as coming to faith.

PRAYER

Lord, grant me to wait for the coming of your salvation in the joyful hope of Simeon and Anna. Help me to welcome it as it is fulfilled in me in whatever way you will, by happiness or by sorrow. Let me see both happiness and sorrow as your light dawning from on high.

JESUS IN THE TEMPLE AGAIN

Jesus Among the Teachers of the Law

THIS INCIDENT HAS captured the imagination of artists through the ages, who show the twelve-year-old Jesus teaching the teachers. This is not what the Gospel says. He was sitting among the teachers, listening to them, and asking them questions. It was his replies and his intelligence—the clarity and directness of the child—that astonished them, rather than his precociousness.

The background to the scene is the devoted practice of pilgrimage. Jerusalem was a real center of pilgrimage, a sort of holy holiday. The biblical custom was three annual pilgrimages to Jerusalem for three great feasts. For the Passover it became so crowded that the theoretical limits of the city, within which the Passover must be celebrated, were extended to include the Mount of Olives. So there was a fair amount of thronging and celebrating crowds.

Didn't You Know?

FOR ME THE most endearing feature of the scene is a touch typical of any twelve-year-old, which Luke has captured perfectly. Anyone who has dealt with children of that age will know their infuriating and worrying habit of disappearing, wrapped up in their own exciting preoccupations, worries, or explorations. When the distracted parents have torn their hair, searched every corner, probably phoned the police, the child will reappear, innocent and bright-eyed, to say, "Didn't you know? I only went frog hunting." It is perfectly clear to the child that this activity was the most obvious thing in the world to do, that anyone of any sense would know exactly where this particular child was to be found, and there was nothing to worry about. This is just what the twelve-year-old Jesus does. Luke is showing us that he was human through and through. Mary, the wise mother, reacts calmly after her three-day worry, and accepts his answer without complaint or cavil. She does not understand all the implications; she merely obediently takes him for what he is, an inquiring youngster.

At the same time, of course, the reader sees where Jesus' center of gravity lies. The English language does not allow the indefiniteness of the Greek, "in my Father's realm, in his territory, about his business, among his friends"—all are included. I am tempted to translate by a phrase that would fit in the Gospel of John, "at my Father's side."

The Adolescent

THE VISIT TO the temple is sandwiched between two brief and sober references to Jesus' hidden life at Nazareth. They contain little information. Both before and after, two elements are repeated, his growth in wisdom and the favor of God. Other factors are mentioned: He lived under his parents' authority, and he grew in maturity and in stature.

The later "Infancy Gospels," documents of the second century embroidered with Christian devotion and imagination, fill out the hidden years with the child Jesus molding clay pigeons and breathing life into them, or—less edifyingly—withering up companions who beat him at games. These were not accepted by the early Church as a true account. The silence of the Gospels is more valuable, for silence has its own worth. The mention of growth is enough to remind us that he was a real boy, youngster, young man. He went through the inquiries, daydreams, doubts, bewilderment, enthusiasms, tenderness, and vigor of every growing child. He will have discovered his own sexuality, too, with all its excitements and heartache.

At the base of his consciousness must have been the growing awareness of his own personality and of his union to his Father, growing in just the way that every child becomes, in unsteady leaps and bounds and unexpected gulps, aware of personal identity. The growth in wisdom did not mean that he was always serious. Many a child shows an almost awesome wisdom and then immediately bursts into inconsequent impishness or laughter.

PRAYER

Jesus, you discovered yourself. You grew in wisdom and maturity.
You knew what it was to obey. No doubt some of the orders of your elders
were unjust and hurtful. You came to share our humanity, its joys
and trials. Grant me always to be open with you and confident,
and to share my humanity with you.

LUKE 3:1–6

COMMUNITY OF REPENTANCE

The Historical Context

LUKE PREFACES HIS account of Jesus' ministry with a roll call of worthies. Each suggests a different aspect of the world history into which Jesus was plunged. The emperor Tiberius Caesar ruled the known world, with its clanking footgear of battle. The Romans were engineers, whose drains, straight roads, aqueducts, and theaters can be seen in Carthage, Constantinople, and Cirencester, making one single, worldwide culture. The same plan of defensive wall and military camp lies visible on the shores of the Dead Sea and the banks of the Tyne. A roman soldier in York had an inscription carved on his tombstone in his native Aramaic. Tiberius himself was a tough general—as a young man he once rode two hundred miles in twenty-four hours—but by this time was leaving most of the affairs of state to his slimy minister, Sejanus.

Locally the Roman power was represented by Pontius Pilate, the longest-serving Roman governor of Judea. His job was to guard the peace and Roman interests in the country, to keep under control the incomprehensible Jews with their odd eating habits, their waste of one day in seven, their contempt for the Olympian gods. Despite the bad press he gets from later Jewish apologists, he must have been a skilled operator, with at least some human qualities, to last so long.

Pilate's opposite number on the Jewish side was the high priest. Caiaphas worked with Pilate for nearly a decade. Pilate mostly kept his watching brief from Caesarea on the coast, while Caiaphas presided over the nation and its seething religious squabbles from his palace in Jerusalem. Annas was his father-in-law, and together they formed the center of a powerful clan of priestly families. With his council, and no doubt his informers, he will have picked up on this charismatic figure who appeared at the crossing point where the road to the east forded the Jordan. In the neighboring territories (where Jesus' ministry began) an insecure dependent sovereignty was held by the three mediocre sons of that hated tycoon, King Herod the Great.

The mere mention of the rulers' names serves to sketch a world of real people going about their own businesses, with their bustling concerns and preoccupations. This was the cauldron of conflicting interests in which John and Jesus appeared.

John the Baptist's Role

IN MARK'S GOSPEL the Baptist simply appears at the Jordan, dressed as the prophet Elijah, describing himself in Isaiah's words as a voice crying out in the desert and offering a baptism of repentance. He is a figure heralding the end of time and God's decisive intervention in world history, warning and offering a chance to shelter from God's wrath in his community of repentance. At the same time, he looks forward to a greater figure who is to come, and points this out as Jesus when he arrives on the scene. The shock waves caused by his call come to expression long after his murder in prison: The crowds have such respect for him that the temple authorities dare not upset them by denying that John was a prophet.

By the time we get to this point in Luke, we know far more about John. John's vocation and sacred quality have served as a basis on which Jesus' vocation and far greater sacred quality are built. He is not an Elijah announcing the end of all things, but is the forerunner of Jesus. So his message prepares for that of Jesus and, later, of the disciples in Acts, for he emphatically preaches repentance and forgiveness. Throughout Luke these are the prerequisites for any approach to Jesus. Although it is stressed that John's career comes to an end before Jesus' public ministry begins, Luke tells us in Acts that John still had disciples years later in Ephesus. So John's ministry, too, had its lasting international flavor, spreading over the Jewish communities of the Mediterranean world. Was it from a Baptist community that the Alexandrian preacher, Apollos, came to Ephesus? Certainly Luke indicates that the concerns of John himself stretched beyond Judaism: *"All humanity* shall see the salvation of God," he adds to the quotation from Isaiah.

PRAYER

Let every valley be filled in, every mountain and hill be leveled, winding
ways be straightened and rough roads made plain. Lord, help me to see
in myself those valleys, those humps, those corners and roughnesses that
need to be corrected if you are to come and make me your own.

THE BAPTIST'S MESSAGE

IN LUKE, THE Baptist's message is given in a much fuller form than in Mark. It has three components: a warning to repent, a warning about the use of money, and pointing to Jesus.

A Warning

THE BAPTIST WARNS that the ax is being laid to the root of the trees, that the Messiah, Christ, is coming, his winnowing fan in his hand to separate the wheat from the chaff. These are warnings that the moment of judgment is at hand. The people would recognize these images as threats of the Day of the Lord. Since the time of the prophets, and particularly of Amos, the people had constantly been warned that the Day of the Lord was approaching. This was to be a visitation from God that would set right the wrongs in the world. The wicked would be punished and the oppressed released from the oppression. At first this was seen on the individual level: The rich who oppressed the poor would be toppled from their comfortable lifestyle. Then it broadens to the national level: Israel as a whole would be punished for its infidelity, a punishment that was seen as fulfilled in the sack of Jerusalem and the dispersion of the nation to Babylon and beyond. Once this has occurred, Israel is in the place of the oppressed, and the Day of the Lord will, at the end of time, reestablish Israel and punish the nations that oppress Israel.

This was the central element in Israel's expectation of the Messiah, or the Christ (Christ is a Greek word, meaning "anointed," the meaning also of the Hebrew word "Messiah"). The Messiah would establish God's sovereignty, rule, or kingship on earth. This would include fulfilling his promises to Israel, his chosen people. John's warning is that it is not enough simply to be members of that people, children of Abraham. Some of the trees may be dead wood that needs to be cut out. In the final harvest there will be chaff fit only for burning, as well as good grain. For the chaff it will be a day of disaster. This warning against complacency is still relevant for Christians today.

A Community of Repentance

JOHN GOES "THROUGH the whole Jordan area" preaching his message of repentance. Mark and Matthew place his preaching "in the desert," alluding to the passage in Isaiah, "Make straight in the desert a highway for our God." But the whole Jordan area, well below sea level, is barren desert apart from the narrow strip of the Jordan River itself. Christian tradition has narrowed the focus of John's preaching to the point where the great road to the east crosses the Jordan itself, a ford that would daily be thronged with travelers and traders of all kinds.

John describes the fruits of repentance in practical terms, and above all in terms of the use of money and resources. He addresses various classes of people, focusing on the temptation that lies nearest at hand for them. Luke is acutely aware of the danger of wealth and of the need to use wealth responsibly and generously. In the biblical world, excess of wealth was expressed in terms of clothing and food. "Festal robes" feature frequently among lists of grand gifts given by powerful people to each other, and excess of food has been a temptation in every age. Tax collectors and soldiers are warned not to exercise their own particular opportunities for exploitation.

John Points to the Christ

JOHN IS ALREADY the perfect example of the Christian teacher. His message of repentance will be that also of the apostles after Pentecost. Another striking element is his humility. He refuses any acclaim for himself and points always to Christ. No Hebrew slave could be obliged to undo his master's sandals (foot washing was not a frequent occupation in those days!), and yet John says he is not worthy even to do this for the Christ. This has even greater poignancy if Jesus had once been John's disciple— an intriguing possibility that cannot be established. The Baptist's words in John could be the motto of any Christian teacher, priest, parent, or educator: "He must grow greater, I must grow less" (John 3:30).

PRAYER
Lord, save me from complacency and self-importance.
Keep me always aware that the greatest Christian dignity is to be a
channel of your grace, to bring others to the appreciation of your love
and to help them embrace your vision.

THE COMING OF THE SPIRIT

John the Baptist Imprisoned

IN MARK AND Matthew we have a full story of the arrest and execution of the Baptist, rather further on in the story. Luke gives a brief mention here of his arrest, and that is the last we hear of him. Luke is keen to show that John's ministry is only preparatory, and that it comes to an end just as Jesus' ministry is about to begin. History is thus divided into three periods, the preparation for Jesus (the Spirit at work in the preparation, as we have seen in the account of Jesus' birth and the events leading up to it), the lifetime of the earthly Jesus, and the life of Jesus through the Spirit in the work of the apostles as they spread the message of Jesus to the ends of the earth. As we shall see, Luke is at pains to show that the life of the Church echoes and mirrors that of Jesus: In the power of his Spirit the apostles preach the same message, work the same miracles, and undergo the same trials of martyrdom.

John does not even appear at the baptism of Jesus. It seems to have been an embarrassment to the early Church that Jesus submitted himself to baptism at the hands of his inferior, John. Mark merely relates the occasion, but Matthew gives a little dialogue between the two. The importance of this dialogue is to show that it is not an action of John upon Jesus, but is a joint action of the two: "It is fitting that *we* should, in this way, do all that righteousness demands," says Jesus. Luke solves the problem by not telling us who baptized Jesus.

The Coming of the Spirit

INDEED, IN THIS Gospel the event can hardly be called the baptism of Jesus. The baptism is hardly more than a timing device for the coming of the Spirit. Just as the beginning of the mission of the apostles is marked, kicked off by the descent of the Spirit at Pentecost, so the mission of Jesus is marked by the descent of the Spirit on him, "while Jesus after his own baptism was at prayer." The reality of the event is stressed by its physical character: The Spirit descends not only "like a dove," as in the other Gospels, but "in a physical form."

In Luke, Jesus is at prayer before all the important events of his life— the transfiguration, the choice of the apostles, the teaching on the Lord's Prayer—as well as the prayer in Gethsemane before the Passion. The same importance of prayer at crucial moments is shown also in the life of the early Christian community gathered together in Jerusalem in the Acts of the Apostles. Particularly the disciples turn to prayer before the beginning of a mission: before the appointment of the twelfth apostle, before the appointment of the seven "deacons," before Paul is sent out on his mission by the community at Antioch. We will also find many lessons in Luke on the quality of prayer and how to pray.

What can be meant by "heaven opened"? This again is scriptural language. At the beginning of the first chapter of Ezekiel, the heaven opens to reveal the scintillating vision of the chariot of God. This is the nearest the Bible gets to giving us a vision of God in person: "The sight was like the glory of the Lord." At the baptism this prepares us for the full divine majesty and authority of the voice proclaiming Jesus as his authorized messenger, the Son of God. So is the stage set for Jesus to begin his mission of bringing God's message to the world.

The Ancestry of Jesus

THE GENEALOGY OF Jesus given by Matthew at the beginning of his Gospel goes back to Abraham. That was the Jewish ancestry of Jesus, son of David, son of Abraham. Here, on the other hand, the ancestry goes back further, to Adam himself, the progenitor of the whole human race. The details—and their differences from Matthew's account—are unimportant. The point being made is that Jesus is of universal significance, not just to Jews but to all people of all races descended from Adam. Salvation is to be proclaimed to them all.

PRAYER
*Lord Jesus, the voice from heaven at your baptism assures us
that you set out on your mission in the full Spirit and power of your
Father. You fill your followers, too, with this Spirit. Grant me confidence
in that Spirit, not in myself, so that I may respond sensitively to your
direction through your own Spirit living in me.*

LUKE 4:1-13

TESTING IN THE DESERT

Preparation

MARK GIVES US a short account of this incident. Jesus was put to the test by Satan in the desert. But the only details are "He was with the wild animals and the angels looked after him." It is the peace of the time of the Messiah, as foretold by Isaiah (11:6): "The wolf will live with the lamb, the panther lie down with the kid." And the angels are fulfilling God's promise in Psalm 91, ". . . to guard you wherever you go."

Luke concentrates much more on the details of the testing. Through his eyes we can see that in the forty days in the desert, Jesus, the Son of God, is undergoing the same testing as Israel, God's son, underwent in the forty years of wandering in the desert after the exodus from Egypt. Only, where Israel so often failed and complained, Jesus remains faithful and true to his Father. The number of forty is often used in the Bible for a period of preparation: not only the forty years of Israel's wanderings while it was being forged into a nation under God's care, but Elijah's forty days and forty nights of preparation in the desert for his encounter with God at Horeb (1 Kings 19:8). The closest parallel of all is the forty days of preparation between the resurrection and the ascension, when the risen Christ is preparing his disciples for their mission. Just as the mission of Jesus begins with a preparation period of forty days, so does the mission of his disciples.

The dialogue between Jesus and the devil is also a reminder that Jesus is undergoing the same testing in the desert as that undergone by Israel in the desert. The dialogue is like a religious discussion between rabbis, each participant setting Bible text against Bible text, as we know from countless rabbinic discussions preserved in contemporary Jewish writings. The first two texts that the devil produces are drawn from the book of Deuteronomy; the third text is from a psalm, but Jesus neatly replies with a text from Deuteronomy, turning the discussion back upon the tempter. The link with the testing of Israel in the desert is that Deuteronomy, the last book of Moses, describes the wanderings and murmurings of Israel in the desert.

The Messianic Mission

AFTER THE DECLARATION of the beginning of his mission with the coming of the Spirit, Jesus withdraws into the desert to prepare. It is a profound occasion of grace, for he is "filled with the Holy Spirit." What was his mission to be? How was he to fulfill his task as Messiah? There were many different aspects of the hopes for the Messiah. The Gospel here shows us Jesus being presented with some of them by the devil. They are false trails, and so temptations that must be resisted.

The first, to turn stones into bread, represents the temptation to material plenty. One hope for the messianic times was a time of perpetual feasting, all play and no work—the easy way out, a shortcut to contentment and physical luxury.

The second temptation, to have power over all the kingdoms of the earth, represents the notion of a powerful kingship, a dictatorship by force. Domination by brute force is often an easy way out. It comes from the thrust in everyday life to dominate and exploit without regard for the rights and feelings of others. As in the story of Adam and Eve, perhaps the basic temptation for all humanity is the temptation to exercise power and independence without caring for the consequences. This is why it results in falling down and worshiping the spirit of evil. Christ's kingship is utterly different from this, a kingship over the heart, which must be won.

Jesus' third temptation, to throw himself down from the temple, represents the power of showing off with "flashy" miracles and self-aggrandizement, very different from the humility and gentleness of Jesus. Jesus worked his miracles in response to need, healing the sick and comforting the disabled, not showing off his own power and the divine protection he might have enjoyed—particularly in the lonely agony of his Passion.

These temptations, given here in a neat and rather formal mode, no doubt recurred for Jesus throughout his life. In the fourth Gospel one can see Luke's second temptation occurring, for instance, in the temptation to accept the offer of kingship (John 6:15). The way of the Son of God was far from luxury, royalty, or popular acclaim.

PRAYER
Lord, help me to see what is your way and what is only mine.
Grant me the wisdom to distinguish your will from my self-deceptions.
Grant me the courage to follow your path.

JESUS AT NAZARETH

AFTER THE DESCENT of the Spirit at his baptism, and a period of withdrawal and assessment in the desert, Jesus at last begins his public ministry with what would today be called a keynote address. Again there is a careful parallel in the Acts of the Apostles: After the descent of the Spirit at Pentecost, Peter makes a great speech, a sort of manifesto. Both speeches begin by explaining the presence of the Spirit in the terms of the ancient prophets. The scene at Nazareth is painted with all Luke's skill and artistry: the dramatic reading from scripture, the calm exposition, the angry response. Jesus throws down a challenge—only to be immediately rejected. The scene is a fuller and more explicit version of the rejection of Jesus by his own people at Nazareth recounted by Mark.

First, he declares that the time of the Spirit has come: "The spirit of the Lord is on me," as in the prophet Isaiah. Jesus himself is seen as a prophet. The prophet's ministry in the power of the Spirit is not to foretell the future but to bring the people back to God's path, and this is what Jesus proceeds to do. There are two particular directions in which his message here points.

Good News to the Poor

THE QUOTATION FROM Isaiah concentrates on captives, the afflicted, the poor, and the oppressed. Throughout his Gospel, Luke will stress that these are the favored children of God, to whom Christ's message is primarily addressed. The shepherds at Bethlehem, Lazarus covered with sores at the rich man's gate, the outcast tax collectors, the executed criminal, are all in different ways the special object of God's care. Luke seems generally more at home in a richer world than do either Mark or Matthew: He uses larger sums of money in his imagery; he mentions bankers, loans, interest rates, and other such high financial matters, which would have left Mark's audience utterly puzzled. Writing to a rich audience, it makes more sense for Luke to underline the danger of wealth and the need to use it rightly, and especially God's care for the poor. In Luke, the beatitudes promise blessedness to the poor now and to those who hunger and thirst now, while Matthew's envisage the poor *in spirit,* and those who hunger and thirst *for righteousness.* So Luke concentrates on the material need, on those who do not know where their next meal is coming from, while Matthew concentrates on moral and spiritual qualities.

Nor is Jesus' message in Luke confined to the financially underprivileged. He has special care for the outcasts and sinners, all those marginalized by polite society. This is one reason Luke is always careful to show that Jesus' message comes to women equally with men: Anna as well as Simeon, Mary as well as Zechariah, the widow of Nain (and her son) as well as Jairus (and his daughter), the woman who lost a coin as well as the man who lost a sheep, the woman who was a sinner as well as the prodigal son.

Good News to the Gentiles

JESUS' PROPHETIC PROCLAMATION makes clear that his message is for the other nations of the world as well as for Israel. Indeed, more than that, he stresses that the chosen recipients of the miracles of the great prophets Elijah and Elisha were Gentiles rather than Jews, Naaman the Syrian rather than any leper in Israel, the widow of Zarephath, "a town in Sidonia," rather than any widow in Israel. Especially in the Gospel of Luke, we see Jesus paying special attention to non-Jews. In Mark and Matthew he has little contact with them. In Luke we find the parable of the good Samaritan (and the Samaritans were hated by the Jews) and the one Samaritan leper who came to thank Jesus after ten lepers were healed. In the parable of the great supper the messengers are sent to invite the outcasts in the city (representing Jerusalem or Judaism); but there is still space and they are sent outside the city to compel the outsiders to come to the feast. The reader is made aware that after Pentecost the second volume of Luke's work will deal with the spread of the gospel to all the nations of the known world. The ground is already being prepared for this.

PRAYER

Lord, you came to bring the good news to all the nations.
The whole world is to be transformed by your message of peace.
Enable me to welcome that message and to spread it even—and
especially—to the harmed and handicapped members of society.

A DAY AT CAPERNAUM

IMMEDIATELY AFTER JESUS' proclamation of his mission he goes down to Capernaum, the lakeside village that will be his home now that he has been rejected by his own townsfolk of Nazareth. There we see a sort of sample day of his ministry, consisting of the cure of a man in the synagogue, the cure of Simon's mother-in-law, and an unspecified number of other cures. In Mark, the day at Capernaum comes considerably earlier than the incident at Nazareth, and this is obviously the original historical order. Luke arranges the events in an order that gives prominence to Jesus' first public appearance during his mission at Nazareth. There Jesus makes the keynote sermon which is a sort of manifesto of the program of his ministry and mission.

A Word of Authority

THE DOMINANT IMPRESSION of Jesus' miracles on the day at Capernaum is one of authority. The authority of his teaching makes a deep impression on the people in the synagogue. Then Jesus confirms this by expelling the unclean spirit merely by his word. It is the authority of his word that makes the deep and astonishing impression: He merely rebukes the unclean spirit. Later Jesus rebukes the fever that has gripped Simon's mother-in-law, and again his word alone suffices to cure her. In the other Gospels he takes her by the hand and raises her up, but in Luke no physical gesture is needed. Again, in the last group of cures, Jesus rebukes the evil spirits and prevents them speaking: No word is to rival his own. Even though they cry out that he is "the Son of God," their proclamation is forbidden, for no one but Jesus and his followers may spread the message.

It is the word of preaching and the message that are being stressed, and indeed at the end of the series of incidents Jesus says he must go to proclaim the good news elsewhere. So it is the force and authority of the proclamation of the good news that is responsible for all these cures. In the Acts of the Apostles the word of Jesus spoken by the disciples in his name will have the same effect of authority and healing. One cannot but reflect on the power the word of God should have in the preaching of the Church today. It must be a healing word as well, curing disorders and driving out evil.

Evil Spirits

THE GOSPELS SHOW many people going around Galilee in the grip of demonic possession. It would be brash to maintain that such possession does not and could not occur. However, in a world of primitive medicine, grave physical distortions and profound mental disorders were attributed primarily to the influence of evil spirits. Anyone who has seen a dear friend in the grip of such agony can sympathize with this description.

Mental disorders are today sometimes cured by prolonged courses of therapy. It may be that what the Gospel describes as an evil spirit yielding to Jesus is the encounter of such a tortured personality with the healing presence of Jesus. So great was his authority and so healing his presence that his word could instantly bring peace and restore the victim to normality. No human personality can have such wondrous, instant effect. But most of us will have met extraordinary people whose personalities can provide a glimmer of understanding of such an experience and of the astonishment it would cause.

Son of God

THE DEMONS HERE call Jesus "Son of God," the first time this title has been used in the ministry of Jesus. The angel at the annunciation had declared that Jesus would be Son of God, and the devil had taunted him with this expression during the temptations in the desert; "If you are the Son of God . . ." Here we begin to see what it means. But this is only a beginning, and its full sense will become gradually clearer. Angels and judges, rulers and Israel itself, are also called "sons of God," and it will be long before human beings acknowledge Jesus as Son of God in a full sense. But to Christians the title has a profound meaning, and Luke is writing for those who already believe in the fullness of Jesus as Son of God.

PRAYER

Lord, grant me to see and treasure the wonder of your healing power in all the distressful situations of life.

LUKE 5:1-11

THE CALL OF FOUR DISCIPLES

THERE MUST HAVE been several stories circulating in the early Christian communities about the call of the first disciples. In Mark, Jesus calls Simon, Andrew, and the two sons of Zebedee as they are tending their fishing nets on the shore of the lake. He just walks along, calls them to follow him, and they go after him, simply drawn by his personality. In the fourth Gospel, John the Baptist (presumably in the Jordan valley) points out Jesus to Andrew and another disciple, who approach Jesus and are won over to believe in him as the Messiah. Then they are joined individually by Simon, Philip, and Nathanael. Luke's story here has a close similarity to the story of the miraculous catch of fish after the resurrection in John 21. There also they fish unsuccessfully all night, then they are guided by Jesus to net a huge haul; the climax of the scene is Jesus' appointment of Peter to feed his sheep. Three times the risen Christ asks Peter whether he loves him and elicits a protestation of loyalty that must surely correspond to Peter's three denials a few days earlier. Luke's story here contains the same hint of admission of failure when Peter falls on his knees to Jesus and confesses that he is a sinner.

The Lake of Galilee

THE LAKE OF Galilee (or Gennesaret, as Luke here calls it) is a placid inland sea some eight miles long and five miles wide at its broadest point. It lies almost seven hundred feet below sea level, the level of the Mediterranean Sea, in a bowl, surrounded by high hills. There are little villages dotted around its shore; Capernaum is one of them. The River Jordan, a slow and muddy little stream, flows into it at the north end, and out of it at the south, down toward the Dead Sea. Being so low, the lake is always warm and has abundance of fish. It has always been the center of a thriving fishing industry carried on by small boats working in family or small village community partnerships. The traditional place of this catch of fish and Peter's call is a couple of miles from Capernaum, at a spot where some warm springs flow into the lake. The fish congregate there, especially in the early spring (which would fit especially the story in John 21, just after the resurrection), and the canny fisherman would know this. It is hardly a mile along the shore from Magdala, the home of Mary Magdalene. The whole shore is studded with memories of Jesus and his ministry.

"I Am a Sinner"

PETER'S REACTION TO the wonderful catch of fish is awe and amazement, expressed in a sense of his own unworthiness to be in the presence of this personality. This is just like the prophet Isaiah, at his call in the temple, when he experiences the vision of God filling the temple and crumples in awareness of his own sinfulness. Especially Luke draws out the truth that awareness and acknowledgment of sin is a primary prerequisite for being called to be a follower of Jesus. So the tax collector Zacchaeus acknowledges that he must return his ill-gotten gains as Jesus calls him. It is only after the good thief has twice admitted that he is getting his just deserts that Jesus promises to take him into paradise. Most Christian rituals and services begin therefore with an admission of sin, by which the Christian is put in the frame of mind to accept Christ again.

"They Left Everything"

IN MARK AND Matthew, when the first disciples are called, they leave their father, their nets, their boat, and their livelihood. But it is only Luke who stresses that they left *everything*. Luke's awareness of the danger of wealth is such that he underlines that the true disciples of Jesus must be wholly free of this distraction. His parable of the rich man and Lazarus shows the dangers of selfishness with wealth. In the parable of the great supper it is the fascination with possessions that distracts the invited guests from taking up the invitation. Again and again the warning is given, so Peter and his companions leave everything to avoid any possible danger from possessions.

PRAYER

Lord, how often is my pride a barrier to your work! Yet I know that
I am prepared to trust others as your representatives precisely because
they know their faults and have no pretensions. Help me to remember
that I am a sinner, yet safe and secure in your mercy.

TWO MIRACULOUS CURES

THE TERRIBLE THING about "leprosy" was the separation from society that it involved. The term is used much more widely in the Bible than in modern medicine. It was not confined to the disease that results in the leper colonies of Africa to which Father Damien and Albert Schweitzer gave their lives, a disease that has almost died out with the advance of medicine. It embraced a whole group of contagious skin infections, and the Bible prescribed that sufferers from these diseases should be isolated from society until they were officially pronounced clean. The rules for diagnosis given in Leviticus 13–14 are impressively careful and thoughtful, though, of course, they lack the exact analysis of modern medicine. In many cases the separation from society must have been more painful than the disease itself. It is moving that Jesus' compassion for the victim of the disease is such that he fearlessly touches him, deterred neither by the risk of infection nor by the biblical rules.

Then, as so often in Luke, there is the little note that he went off to pray. This prayer of Jesus comes between the two miracle stories, as a reminder of what Jesus is really about. The acclaim of the crowds is not the mainspring of his action. Jesus returns constantly to prayer as the background of all his actions. This is the more striking as Luke here recounts it: In the midst of all the acclaim and the spread of the message, there is only one relationship that is of real importance to Jesus. He turns his back on the popular success to return to the Father in prayer.

Healing and Forgiveness

LUKE HAS TAKEN over the story of the healing of the "paralytic" from Mark. Again the "paralytic" is not exactly paralytic in the modern sense of someone unable to move; it means, rather, "bedridden." There are two cures, which reflect on each other, a physical and a spiritual cure. The combination of the two, side by side, or, rather, intertwined, shows that Jesus could heal the one ailment as easily as the other. The two are put together at several levels. In the messianic renewal the Messiah will come to abolish all evil and bring back the peace and blessedness of paradise, when both these evils are to be abolished together. So Jesus' miracles are prophetic signs of the beginning of that renewal. At another level, in the primitive prescientific world sin was often thought to be the cause of illness, a connection Jesus explicitly rejects in the case of the man born blind (John 9:3), but which no doubt remained strong in the popular mentality. Both are signs that Jesus is acting with the sovereign power of God, for God alone can forgive sin and God alone has free power over human life.

The Power of the Lord

LUKE ADDS A particular awe to the story by his statement "The power of the Lord was there so that he should heal." It is not clear who "the Lord" is in this case. Is it God or Jesus? Who does the healing, God or Jesus? One of the special marks of Luke's use of "the Lord" is that one cannot tell whether it is God or Jesus; the ambiguity shows the growing understanding of the mystery of Jesus in the Christian community during the course of the first generation of Christians. At the conclusion of the story of the Gerasene demoniac in Luke's version even more explicitly than in Mark, "God" and "Jesus" seem to be the same: " 'Go back home and report all that *God* has done for you.' So the man went off and proclaimed throughout the city all that *Jesus* had done for him." In whose power is this miracle done? Jesus' awesome power is given particular respect by Luke, without making clear whether it is Jesus' own power or divine power in him. It almost seems a sort of *mana,* a kind of supernatural power: Everyone tries to touch him and be healed because "power came out of him that cured them all" (6:19). When the woman with a hemorrhage touches him, Jesus says, "I felt that power had gone out from me" (8:46). It is a power he passes on to his followers when he sends them out: "He gave them power and authority over all devils and to cure diseases" (9:1).

PRAYER
Grant me an appreciation of your power. You became a man to show us the power and the caring love of God in human form. You can make me whole again if only I will give myself to you.

A FEAST WITH SINNERS

LUKE NOW WELDS together three scenes: the call of Levi, a meal with tax collectors, and the question about fasting. Immediately after his call, Levi makes a great feast for Jesus in his house. It is part of Luke's cheerful style that he loves a party with plenty of lively dialogue. There can, of course, be good and bad parties, as we learn especially from Luke's parables. The rich fool who had to enlarge his barns, and the rich man who neglected Lazarus, both feasted every day but got little joy of it in the end. On the other hand, the shepherd who sought out his lost sheep and the woman who found her lost coin each invited friends and neighbors for a merry party to celebrate. Another parable warns that a party is not simply an occasion for inviting friends who will repay the hospitality; it must be an occasion for generosity and winning friends in heaven. For the guests a party can be an occasion of humility, in not choosing the best places but waiting to be called up higher. Luke often uses a dinner as a scene for teaching, not least the Last Supper, where he gathers together several important teachings of Jesus.

The Call of Levi

THE BREVITY OF this call-narrative is important. Its very starkness is the most striking feature: Jesus simply summons the tax collector and the tax collector follows, leaving everything. There is no introduction, no preparation, no reasoning. Capernaum was the first town inside the province of Galilee after crossing the border (the River Jordan) on the main road from Syria and the east. It was, no doubt, an important customs post, and there would be entry taxes to pay. But we are left on our own to imagine Levi sitting at his custom table beside the dusty road. All Luke shows is that the personality of Jesus is such that the call is compelling. This must be another illustration of that extraordinary authority of the word of Jesus which we have seen healing the sick and curing the possessed.

There is another aspect of Jesus' fearless authority here too. Tax collectors were outcasts from society, especially from decent religious society. Tax collectors are, from the nature of their job, not popular; the job requires a certain unyielding severity. Taxation itself was a fairly recent innovation in Palestine and the institution itself would still have been disliked. Under the Roman system it was worse, for they worked on something very similar to a commission basis: Once they had filled their quota, the rest went into their own pockets. Worst of all, they worked for the hated Roman oppressors. So, all in all, to call a tax collector into the group spreading the good news of God's kingship was a bold gesture. One can imagine the gasps of astonishment from the rest of the group. One can imagine also the thrilled gratitude of the tax collector at breaking out of the vicious circle into which he had bound himself.

The shocking nature of what has happened is underlined at the party that follows. The Pharisees were the conventional representatives of a devoted search for God. Nowadays we may be critical or even mocking of their methods of seeking God, of their arrogance and hypocrisy, and (most of all) of the superstitious exactitude of their observance. But there is ample evidence in rabbinic stories that they were aware of all these dangers, and could even laugh at themselves.

Conversion

THIS WHOLE SECTION in Luke demands that we reflect on the nature of something that Luke emphasizes in all his call-narratives, conversion. Levi leaves "everything" to follow Jesus; in an instant he gives up his whole way of life. In the conversation at the supper, Jesus adds that he has come not just to call sinners, but to call sinners *to repentance*. The Greek word means "a change of mind-set." It consists in the adoption of a whole new set of values. This is illustrated by the abandonment of such conventional ways to holiness as fasting; Jesus wants to emphasize the joy of coming to him. So he uses such images as the merriment of a wedding feast, the joy of harvest time. This is reinforced by the other images: You cannot patch an old piece of clothing with new cloth, or put new wine into skins already soaked in old wine.

PRAYER

Lord, grant me to reexamine my values, the ways in which I think I am seeking you. Lead me to a true conversion, so that my whole way of life flows from the joy in your kingship.

SABBATH CONTROVERSIES

LUKE NOW GIVES us two stories of Jesus' confrontation with the Jewish authorities about the sabbath. In each, the point of the story is Jesus' authority. Just as his teaching with authority amazed the onlookers, so his action expresses the same authority. Luke's audience was not primarily interested in the Jewish Law, and for him the special purpose of these stories is to illustrate the personality of Jesus.

Plucking Corn on the Sabbath

THERE WAS NOTHING wrong with walking through a cornfield and plucking a few ears of corn to eat. The Law allowed plucking corn by hand in a neighbor's field, but not use of a sickle; the difference presumably is between satisfying passing hunger and garnering corn. The tricky point in this instance was the sabbath, for threshing was forbidden on the sabbath, and rubbing the corn in their hands was construed by the Pharisees as threshing.

Luke's view of the incident can best be seen by a comparison of his telling of it with Mark's and Matthew's. Mark gives here Jesus' saying, "The sabbath was made for man, not man for the sabbath." It is an argument within the Jewish Law. For Luke's Gentile audience, such a controversy had little relevance. So he omits this saying; his Gentile audience was not interested in the relative importance of the Jewish sabbath observance. Luke's interest is in the supreme authority of the Son of Man. Luke inserts "took" into the way Mark describes David's action in the house of God, and so stresses David's commanding authority: "He went into the house of God *and took* the loaves of the offering and ate them and gave them to his followers." For Luke, David is the precedent for Jesus' right to override petty rules of the Law. One is reminded of the story in Acts when in a vision Peter sees clean and unclean food together let down in a sheet from heaven. To Peter's indignant surprise, he is told that there is no such thing any longer as clean and unclean food: All food created by God is clean. So now Jesus does not ask permission. He does not have to justify his actions. He is simply the Lord of the sabbath.

Cure of a Man with a Withered Hand

THE SECOND STORY pairs with the first. The parallelism (and Luke likes parallels) is already suggested by the openings, "one sabbath," "On another sabbath." The original issue in this second story must be whether it was legitimate to cure on a sabbath. This could be construed as being work, and therefore against the command of keeping the sabbath free for the Lord. Mark puts it very simply: It is a matter of Jesus' sympathy and pity for the sufferer. He is angered and grieved at the hardness of heart of his opponents, who just sit there, waiting for him to put a foot wrong, and impervious to the man's plight. Matthew, who is always concerned about the Law and keeping within its bounds, makes the incident into a legal controversy by introducing a statement of principle: If it is legal to pull an ox out of a pit on the sabbath (and not all authorities agreed that it was), it must be legal to heal a human being.

Luke, as we have seen, was not interested in the Jewish Law. He retells the story, changing a few details. No doubt these changes were unconscious, and all accord with his conception of Jesus' imperious authority. First Luke adds that Jesus went into the synagogue *to teach;* he was not there as a simple worshiper. Then he adds that Jesus knew the thoughts of those who were watching to catch him out. The mention of Jesus' anger and grief at their attitude has disappeared; to Luke Jesus is above getting upset about such things. On the contrary, Luke adds a slight touch that makes the man's plight worse: It is his *right* hand, his working hand, which is withered.

The grandeur of the occasion is also stressed by the man's stance. In Mark, Jesus merely tells the man to get up into the middle. In Luke, Jesus tells the man to get up and *take his stand* in the middle, adding "and he came forward and stood there" out in the middle of the synagogue, so that we can have no doubt about the public nature of the miracle. So all this shows another occasion of the power of the Lord being there to work miracles.

PRAYER

Lord, as a human being you showed an awesome power of command over all creation, human and animal, natural and beyond nature. Grant me to appreciate that this gives hardly an inkling of your divine power, always present and always at work.

THE CHOICE OF THE TWELVE

The Prayer of Jesus

BEFORE SOME ESPECIALLY important occasion in Jesus' life, Luke always shows him going off to pray. This time Jesus spent the whole night in prayer, an indication of the importance of this moment. But it cannot be a mere exterior event that leads him to prayer, like the panic prayer at the last minute before an examination, an interview, a driving test. The prayer of Jesus is a return to his Father, a moment of peace, when he can be truly himself, and linked to the "ground of his being." Following Jesus, every Christian yearns for this moment, when passing worries are put aside, and we face in awe and wonder the deepest of all realities, whom we call God. It is a moment of reverence and fear, but a moment also of confidence and trust, a moment of losing self and of finding self again, enriched and enhanced.

The Twelve

WE DO NOT know very much about the Twelve, not even all their names, for the names of the Twelve (though always twelve in number) vary slightly in the different lists. Peter is the spokesman and leader, but otherwise, apart from James and John, the sons of Zebedee, none of them plays any individual part in the first three Gospels. From their names it has been deduced that some of them were nationalists, for Simon, John, Matthew, and Judas are names of the great leaders of the Maccabean revolt against the Syrian monarchy in the second century before Christ. The Syrian king had tried to replace Jewish religious belief and customs with the Greek conventional religion that prevailed all over the rest of his empire, only to encounter fierce opposition roused by these leaders. It may have been that the names of these leaders continued in the Galilean families as a sign of religious fidelity, and that this was what made them responsive to Jesus' call.

Many attempts have been made over the centuries to probe into the mind of Judas, "who became a traitor." One interpretation sees the name as a sign that he first became a disciple in the belief that Jesus was a nationalist leader like Judas the Maccabee, and would lead a rebellion to throw off the Roman yoke. On discovering that he had misjudged Jesus' messianic claims, he became disillusioned and betrayed him. More poignant is the truth that Judas is the symbol of the tragedy of Jesus. The tragedy of the cross is that Jesus dies alone, deserted even by his chosen followers, his attempts to found God's kingdom seemingly in tatters. From the human point of view, he has failed. He failed to convert the crowds in Galilee. The twelve chosen supporters on whom he relied all deserted him. Worst of all, one of them actually turned him in. The mustard seed appeared to have rotted to nothing in the ground. He could boast no human success at all. He could rely only on his fidelity to his Father's will. It is this love and faithfulness that is the secret of the cross.

Apostles

THE TWELVE ARE the twelve foundation stones of the new Israel, corresponding to the twelve tribes of Israel. Matthew tells us that they will sit on twelve thrones, judging the twelve tribes of Israel. The mere existence of this body of twelve is one of the most important signs that Jesus meant to found a new Israel, a new people of God. Chosen from the larger body of Jesus' disciples, their name means "sent out," and later tradition ascribes to each of them a separate region of the world to which they each brought the message of Jesus. So there is a strong tradition, for instance, that Thomas was the apostle to India. When it comes to the appointment of a substitute for Judas in Acts 1, the qualifications are that he should have been with Jesus right through his ministry, and that he should be a witness to the resurrection. We cannot today be apostles in the sense of the original Twelve, but if we would do the work of Christ and bring the message of Jesus to others, we must first and always spend ample time in prayer with him.

PRAYER

Lord Jesus, if I am to be your apostle, grant me to know you. Grant me the love to come close to you in prayer, and the devotion to persevere in that prayer, buoyed up by the joy of knowledge of you and of your resurrection.

THE BEATITUDES

BOTH THE GOSPEL writers who have an extended sermon early in Jesus' ministry begin with a series of beatitudes. Matthew so starts his great Sermon on the Mount, and Luke the corresponding "Sermon on the Plain" (so called because "he stopped at a piece of level ground" to give the instruction, 6:17). The "beatitude" is a well-known biblical formula, used frequently in the Old Testament, to pronounce God's blessing on certain classes of people or on certain achievements, a sort of divine congratulation: "How blessed the nation whose God is the Lord."

In Matthew, the eight beatitudes provide a list of spiritual attitudes required for the kingdom of heaven. They form almost a checklist of conditions of entry, virtues any Christian must strive for who wishes to live under the sovereignty of God. The beatitudes in Luke are shorter, fiercer, and more paradoxical. There are only four instead of eight, but they are balanced by four "woes," threats against those who disregard them and lack the qualities mentioned. They are phrased more piercingly and directly: not "blesssed are *those* who . . ." but straight to the reader or audience, "blessed are *you* who . . ." They are blows between the eyes, direct and challenging. The most important difference is that in Luke's version Jesus does not praise spiritual qualities ("blessed are the poor *in spirit* . . . who hunger and thirst *for uprightness"*), but paradoxically pronounces blessed by God those who seem most unfortunate and most deserted of society, those who are poor, those who are hungry *now*, those who are weeping *now*. God's special regard is on those whom the world most rejects and who are worst treated by their fellows and by circumstances. On the other hand, the "woes" give a warning to those who are normally considered the most fortunate of society, those who enjoy the good things of this world.

Reversal of Values

THE BACKGROUND OF much of Luke's Gospel must be a comfortable society that needs to be shaken out of its comfort. They are satisfied with their wealth, their plenty, and their laughter. Again and again in the Gospels we are given the disturbing message that God's values are not the same as human values. There is just a different scale.

Two other consequences flow from this presentation of the beatitudes. Firstly, a reassurance to the unfortunate that they have the special care and regard of God. The poor, the hungry, the deprived, the bereaved, may seem to be deserted by God, but in fact they enjoy special favor. It is not easy to see how this is so, especially when one is personally in this position. Is this favor of God just a promise of "pie in the sky" in the future? Is God testing out these favorites? Is God pruning them to make them bear more fruit? If we trust the teaching of John, that the Christian already enjoys eternal life, that Christ dwells in us now, there must be more to the favor of God than just a promise for the future. The trials must be the strengthening of a present personal relationship. It often needs a very strong faith to see this.

The second consequence is a warning that also comes often in the Gospel: Wealth and resources are a dangerous responsibility. The parable of the dishonest steward is clear enough that money must be used to make friends in heaven—in whatever way that may be done.

Persecution

THE TWO GOSPELS agree over the final beatitude, that persecution brings blessedness to the follower of Christ. Following the thrust of their other beatitudes, one may see that the angle is slightly different: Matthew is encouraging the Christian to see perseverance in persecution as a virtue, while Luke is reassuring the Christian that the persecuted will have their reward. Persecution—wild beasts and burning at the stake—was not only for the early Church. We have known enough martyrs in Africa, China, and Europe this century. Even short of bloodshed, to live by Christian principles often draws mockery, taunts, and even material disadvantage.

FOR MEDITATION
"For Christ I have accepted the loss of all other things, and look on them all as filth if only I can gain Christ" (Philippians 3:8).

DEMANDS OF DISCIPLESHIP

THE BEATITUDES HAVE given a basic outline sketch of those who are and are not included in God's kingdom. There follows a commentary and expansion on the demands of discipleship, with a repeated insistence that it is not enough to repay others what they give to you. This was the Golden Rule, a moral principle that existed long before Jesus, and was well known in both Greek and Hebrew literature. It occurs in a popular rabbinic story about two first-century sages, Shammai and Hillel. A prospective follower came to Shammai and asked to be taught the whole Law while he stood on one leg. Shammai, insulted at this absurdity, sent him off with a flea in his ear. Next he went to Hillel and made the same request. Hillel replied with the Golden Rule, "What is hateful to yourself, do not do to your neighbor." For Luke, though the Golden Rule is included, this is not enough.

Fours

WHAT SEEMS AT first a random collection of sayings takes shape if we realize that Luke is thinking in fours. There were four beatitudes and four woes. Now there comes a whole series of fours expressing the excessive demands of Christian discipleship. It is no good pretending that Christianity is merely reasonable, good behavior.

First come four paradoxes (love, do good, bless, pray for) on returning good for evil. These are quiet, interior intentions and attitudes. But they soon spring into action and are reinforced by another four (to anyone who slaps, to anyone who takes, to everyone who asks, from someone who takes). All these involve abandoning natural human rights, and human nature shrieks out against them. Of the four, the first pair demands that Christians positively cooperate with those who infringe their human rights, the second pair instructs followers of Christ not to seek to put right wrongs done to them. These four simply wipe out any claim that Christianity is a reasonable religion: Following Christ goes far beyond that.

Yet it is after this quartet that Luke throws in the reasonable and less demanding Golden Rule, as though for good measure. This is an interesting instance of the different arrangement of material in the two sermons: Matthew gives the Golden Rule at the beginning of his summing up at the conclusion of the Sermon on the Mount; in Luke's arrangement it comes in as an extra after the far more demanding previous reactions to abuse of human rights.

Beyond Reason

AS IF THE lesson had not been sufficiently stressed, Luke next gives a trio of ways in which the generosity of a Christian must exceed the calculations of the reasonable person who expects a return for a favor. "You scratch my back and I'll scratch yours" obtains in many spheres, from calling in political or business favors to lending clothes for a party. In Luke's world his teaching would have struck at the heart of the regular system of patronage and *amicitia* (literally "friendship," but in fact more like bargaining) on which politics in the civilized Roman world were built: Every "boss" had his "clients," and the "big bosses" traded "favors" with each other. This parity of bargaining is not the way of Christ. Luke drives this home by three verses similarly constructed (v. 32 on love, v. 33 on doing good, v. 34 on lending), pulled together by the final three-in-one of v. 35 (love, do good, lend).

The section ends with the most devastating demand of all, to be compassionate as the Father is compassionate—but here there is a reward attached. The meaning of this demand for absolute compassion can be learned from a comparison with the way Matthew expresses it; "Be *perfect* just as your heavenly Father is perfect." Luke sees the Father's perfection as lying in compassion, and indeed this kind of generous and overflowing love comes to expression time and again in his Gospel as the most important of all ideals. The Father is always forgiving, always welcoming back, always seeking what is lost. Luke explains what is meant by means of another quartet, two negative and two positive: Do not judge, do not condemn; forgive, and give. At any rate, there is a crumb of natural comfort that these have their reciprocal reward!

PRAYER

So this, my God, is the meaning of your Son's generosity. I cannot take my stand on human rights, but must be unreasonably generous as you yourself are generous, ludicrously compassionate, and forgiving.

PARABLES

THE SERMON ON the Plain concludes, as does Matthew's Sermon on the Mount, with a clutch of parables, imagery to drive home the lesson and the inspiration that lies behind them, the example of Jesus himself. The Sermon on the Plain is less a blueprint for various activities of a Christian's life than a challenge to go beyond conventional natural morality. The "do-as-you-would-be-done-by" principle of the Golden Rule is no more than a rule for conduct that natural good sense could formulate, the product of fairness and educated self-interest, neat and well-balanced. If you follow this principle, you comfortably know the limits that can be placed on the demands made on you. The devastating challenge of the generosity demanded by the Sermon on the Plain is that its basic principle is a negation of self-interest. Jesus' saying in Luke, "Be compassionate as your Father is compassionate," like Matthew's "Be perfect as your Father is perfect," destroys all comfortable limit. There can be no limits to a compassion that is modeled on that of the Father, just as there can be no limits to the forgiveness prayed for and promised by "Forgive us our trespasses as we forgive those who trespass against us."

Two Images of Criticism

OF THE FOUR parables that conclude Luke's Sermon, the first two discourage criticism of others. The image of the blind leaders is used by Matthew to attack the Pharisees, and possibly Luke has the same meaning, envisaging the blind leaders as Pharisees without actually saying so. Is he implying that those who criticize Christians for deserting Pharisaic practices are leading their disciples to disaster? This may be also the context of the next saying, that the disciple is not above his master. In Matthew, this is applied to persecution: If the master is persecuted, the disciple should expect to be persecuted also, and Luke may envisage the same application.

The second parable, the splinter and the log, with its cheerful exaggeration and neatly reversed order (splinter/log // splinter/log // log/splinter) also discourages criticism of others. The contrast of the two original words increases the wit of the saying: The "splinter" is hardly more than a wisp of straw, whereas the "log" is really a main weight-bearing beam of a house's roof, a massive great piece of timber. But we all know how easy it is to criticize the faults of others, and that it is often the faults to which we ourselves are most prone which annoy us most in others. Indeed, noticing a particular fault in a companion is almost a reason for looking out for that fault in oneself.

The Fruit of the Trees

LUKE APPLIES THE contrast between the fruit of the trees rather differently from Matthew. In Matthew's context it is a means of judging whether the message of a prophet is true and of eliminating false prophets. In Luke it may be another warning against uncharitable and judgmental speech. Alternatively it may be a pair with the final parable, an encouragement to take action on the principles outlined in the Sermon.

The Two Houses

THE CONTRAST OF the two houses is attractively painted by Luke, with much more vigor than Matthew; he always depicts work imaginatively. The man goes digging industriously away, right down to the rock—perhaps too enthusiastically: Is it really necessary to put down another foundation stone once one has hit the rock? The rain and the winds described by Matthew have disappeared, perhaps because in the Near East no rain and no wind is really strong enough to knock down a house. However, a river in flood (in Luke's version) could certainly do this. A flash flood after rains could easily wash away a house incautiously built during the summer in a sandy riverbed. I once nearly experienced the same in a car on the barren shore of the Dead Sea as a flash flood came hurtling down a wadi from the hills behind.

PRAYER
Help me, Lord, to avoid the hypocrisy of claiming high standards and then not bearing their fruit in action. Let me always seek your standards and be straightforward in trying to put them into action.

Two Prophetic Cures

IN HIS KEYNOTE speech at Nazareth, Jesus had reminded his audience of Elijah's cure of Naaman, the Syrian army chief, and of Elisha's visit to the widow of Zarephath, and had promised to fulfill such a prophetic mission. These two miracles, for the Gentile military man and the widow, show just that.

The Centurion's Servant

THIS IS AN especially important event in Luke's Gospel, a contact between Jesus and a non-Jew, which was the first of many. In Mark's Gospel there is very little contact between Jesus and Gentiles, only the celebrated encounter with the Syro-Phoenician woman whose faith wins her daughter's healing (Mark 7:24–30). The story given here by Luke does not occur in Mark, but is given also by Matthew. It has close links also with the "second sign at Cana" in John, when Jesus cures the sick son of a royal official at Capernaum—also without going near the sick boy, but simply rewarding the faith of the father, who believes Jesus' word. Again, in that case, the boy was cured at the moment Jesus' promise was given.

All these stories may well be based on the same oral tradition of a cure by Jesus of a sick child of a Gentile parent, who is brought to health by Jesus' response to the faith of the parent, without Jesus ever going near the sufferer. The slight variations between the different versions would give a fascinating glimpse into the way the stories were handed down by word of mouth in the primitive Christian communities. The circumstances varied and developed, but the essentials remained the same.

Luke was also aware of the parallel between this approach of the first Gentile to Jesus and the approach to Peter of the first Gentile to join the Christian community after the resurrection. Both are centurions, both send messengers, both have deserved well of the Jewish people, both are congratulated and receive a favorable response, Jesus and Peter (in their respective stories) going back with the messengers. In bringing out these parallels, Luke is showing the great significance of this first meeting: It is the beginning of the approach of the Gentiles to Christ. But it is surely also significant that Jesus does not yet go as far as Peter: He does not enter into the Gentile centurion's house.

There is one interesting difference in the versions of Jesus' reply given by Matthew and Luke. In Matthew, Jesus says, *"In no one* in Israel have I found faith as great as this."* According to Luke, he says, *"Not even* in Israel have I found faith as great as this."* In Greek the difference is only two letters. In the buildup of Matthew's Gospel, from Herod's massacre of the children of Bethlehem onward, the Gentiles are as responsive as the Jews are unresponsive. Luke, on the other hand, is at pains to show that at least some of the Jews responded with faith. Jesus (and later, Paul) turns to the Gentiles only after some of the Jews have been received into the new People of God, and so have brought fulfillment to the promises of God to Israel.

The Son of the Widow of Nain

THE STORY ENDS with Jesus being hailed as a great prophet. "God has visited his people" shows the excitement of the people at their renewed experience of prophecy after centuries of absence, when God seemed to be silent among them. Jesus is recognized as a second Elijah, for there is an extraordinary similarity between this story and the story of Elijah raising the only son of the widow who befriended him at Zarephath (1 Kings 17). The suggestion is strengthened by Jesus' mention of this widow in his speech at Nazareth.

It would, however, be a great mistake to think of Jesus going around Galilee, looking for neat parallels to the Old Testament. Jesus traveled around, spreading the good news of the kingdom and responding with love and pity to the needs of the people and situations he met. Luke also emphasizes this point by the warmth with which he tells the stories. It was the disciples afterward who saw the significance of his actions in terms of the biblical forebears, and told the stories in such a way that these parallels would be perceived.

PRAYER

Lord, no matter how desperate the trouble I am in, you always have the solution. Let me turn to you in confidence and wait in hope for your solution.

REFLECTIONS ON JOHN THE BAPTIST

THIS PASSAGE IS crucial for the understanding of Jesus' miracles. The early preaching of John the Baptist had made clear that he was expecting a messiah of fire and judgment, one who would put an ax to the root of the tree that needed cutting down, who would separate the wheat from the chaff and burn up the waste. Now he is off in prison on the far side of the Dead Sea, in Herod's remote fortress of Machaerus. He is troubled at the news of Jesus, for Jesus does not seem to be acting as "the one who is to come" should act. No fire and judgment, no ax to the root, no winnowing fan. So he sends messengers to ask Jesus what is going on.

In reply to the messengers Jesus quotes Isaiah, from two passages, Isaiah 35:5 or 61:1. The burden of the quotation is to show that Jesus' activity does in fact fulfill the prophecies, not perhaps the prophecies of which John was thinking, but other parts of the prophets. The expectation of the Messiah varied considerably; the story of the temptations of Jesus in the desert shows him being presented with one after another of the views of the Messiah which he rejects as not the way of the Lord. "The one who is to come" was pictured quite differently by different groups of the Jews. A warlord? A priest-king? A liberator? A custodian of the Law? A figure appearing mysteriously in the desert? The usher of the final cataclysm? Jesus' answer here shows John the Baptist what the Messiah was truly to be. His actions were prophetic symbols of the end of death, pain, sickness, misery, poverty. This was the good news brought by Jesus.

Summary on John the Baptist

JOHN THE BAPTIST is here shown as the greatest of the prophets, and more than that: He was the messenger (the Greek word is the same as "angel") preparing the way for the Lord. The identity of this Lord is left deliberately ambiguous: It could be either the Lord God or the Lord Jesus. But, by narrating John's arrest before the baptism of Jesus, Luke has insisted that the age of the Baptist was over before the age of Jesus began.

He prepared a people of repentance for the Lord, but concluded his mission before the kingdom itself began to be manifested. This is why the least in the kingdom of God is greater than he.

In another sense there is continuity between John and Jesus and the disciples. All are prophets, filled with the Spirit. The message of repentance is preached by both Jesus and John, and then again by the apostles in the early speeches of Acts. The parallelism between John and Jesus had been stressed in the infancy narratives. It is made clear again in the application of the short parable of the children in the marketplace: "We played the pipes for you, and you wouldn't dance; we sang dirges, and you wouldn't cry." They are satisfied by neither merriment nor mourning, but cavil at each equally. The singing of dirges corresponds to John's ascetic lifestyle, and the merriment to Jesus' feasting with tax collectors and sinners.

Luke does, however, make the distinction that will be increasingly important as it comes to the Passion. All the people (and for "people" Luke carefully uses the Greek word, which indicates not just a large crowd but the People of God, the true Israel) responded to John's message of repentance by accepting baptism. It was only the Pharisees and lawyers who thwarted God's plan by refusing. In fact, the Jewish historian Josephus tells us that Herod Antipas arrested John precisely because he was afraid of John's influence with the people, fearing that John would stir up a movement of rebellion among the people. This popularity—or perhaps reverence would be a better word—is seen when the temple authorities challenge Jesus' high-handed action in the temple. He replies by challenging them to explain the origin of John's authority. They dare not deny that his authority was from God, for fear of repercussions from the people.

The same distinction between the leaders and the people will be seen in Jesus' case at the crucifixion, when the leaders alone will jeer at Jesus, while all the people go home, beating their breasts in penitence.

PRAYER

Lord, teach me how to combine repentance with cheerfulness, since you call for both. Help me to know that my weakness is made strong with your strength.

THE WOMAN WHO WAS A SINNER

THIS FIRST OF Luke's wonderful stories of repentance shows us what to make of the distinction between the Pharisees and sinners. Simon the Pharisee, though he has invited Jesus, has neglected even the decencies of hospitality: Not only has he failed to provide the normal comforts of the cloakroom (in a hot and dusty country a foot wash was a necessity, not so much to remove dust as to make a deodorant oil superfluous!), he has not even greeted Jesus properly. By contrast, the woman lavishes every care on him. Not mere water, but expensive ointment in an expensive jar. Not his head, but his feet. Not a kiss to the face, but his feet covered with kisses.

Jesus himself shows a lovely delicacy. First, he accepts patiently the neglect from his host. Secondly, he does not protect his own good name or his person by thrusting aside contact with the sinful woman. He does not interrogate the woman, ask her her sins or humiliate her in any way; he simply accepts her devotion and her love.

Jesus the Prophet

THE REALITY OF the prophet contrasts markedly with what the onlookers expect from a prophet. It is already important that they are expecting him to behave as a prophet, for Luke presents Jesus as a prophet, and more than a prophet. A prophet is one who sees the reality of things as God sees it, through—so to speak—God's spectacles, and communicates this reality to human beings. The prophet sees into reality more deeply than ordinary people, judging what the real issues and values are. Humanity being what it is, more often than not this message involves correction, so that the prophet's message is seldom welcome or expected, but strikes a chord in the depths of the conscience. The prophet's message is self-authenticating: Once it is pronounced, it is seen to be correct. So on this occasion the onlookers expect the prophet to see through the outward appearance to the human reality behind it. And this is just what Jesus—to their surprise—does; but he sees deeper than they expect or like.

The Parable of the Two Debtors

THE KERNEL OF the story is found in the dialogue. This centers on the parable of the two debtors. The message of the incident is that the woman's generous love earns her forgiveness; she is forgiven much because she loves much. This is complemented by the message in the parable. There the greater generosity of the creditor's forgiveness earns greater love from the man who is more deeply in debt. The love and the forgiveness are the other way round. However, this lack of balanced logic has itself a message: In fact the two, love and forgiveness, are intertwined—love leads to forgiveness and forgiveness leads to love. Each intensifies the other.

Behind the Story

THERE HAS BEEN considerable discussion about whether this story is based on the same incident as the story of the anointing of Jesus at Bethany. There is the same anointing with precious ointment by a woman at a supper, with a rebuke from Jesus to the onlookers. The three Gospels of Matthew, Mark, and Luke also all agree that the host was named Simon and that the jar was made of precious alabaster. There are one or two oddities in Luke's story: Anointing the head was the normal custom, as in Mark and Matthew, but anointing the feet has distinct drawbacks—it makes them sticky, so that the dust adheres all the more! Did the original of the Lucan story present the woman only as washing Jesus' feet with her tears, and then the anointing and the precious alabaster jar slip in from the anointing at Bethany as a further sign of her loving attentiveness?

Traditionally the woman has been regarded as a prostitute, on the grounds that she "had a bad name in the town." In fact the reason for her bad reputation is nowhere stated. Nor in the Gospel story is she identified as Mary Magdalene.

PRAYER

Lord, increase in me that love which brings your forgiveness, and by your forgiveness increase in me that love still further.

THE WOMEN WITH JESUS

LUKE IS ABOUT to give us one of the two major parables he takes over from Mark: the parable of the sower. In Mark this is the dividing line between Jesus' preaching to the masses and his more private instruction and preparation of his little group of disciples. It is preceded by an extended Marcan passage that shows that Jesus was widely rejected: The Pharisees accused him of casting out evil spirits by being in league with Beelzebul, the prince of devils; even his own family failed to understand him, and thought he was out of his mind. In Mark the parable of the sower is a reflection on this rejection.

In Luke the situation is quite different, and this will affect the meaning of the parable for Luke's readers. Both immediately before and after the parable Luke shows us a loyal audience, so that the parable is enveloped in a favorable atmosphere. Before the parable comes the little notice that Jesus went around the towns and villages proclaiming the good news— presumably with the same success as we have already seen. He is accompanied by two groups of disciples, the central group of the Twelve, and the women, who will also witness his death and burial. Two of them, the Magdalene and Joanna, will also be the first to receive the news of his resurrection. Now we are told that they ministered to him, and the same verb is used as in Acts 6, where it refers to the Seven who minister to the needs of the poor of the young community.

Women in Luke

THIS IS ANOTHER instance of Luke's quite deliberately pairing up women with men. In Christianity, women have equal standing with men. The subjects of the miraculous cures by Jesus, and later by the apostles in the early chapters of Acts, are equally women and men. Women just as much as men receive the divine message and call; indeed, in the parallel of Zechariah and Mary, Mary is the clear winner! Parables are about women as well as men: A man loses his sheep, a woman loses her coin. In the early community of Jerusalem, women are constantly mentioned and brought into prominence. Women as well as men are inspired by the Spirit to prophesy. As Paul travels around, women are often the leaders of the group or community who receive him. (This is reflected in the greetings at the end of Paul's letters, especially to the Romans. There women stand at the head of the household in which the Christians meet for worship. Paul even calls a woman, Junia or Julia, an apostle.) At Ephesus both Priscilla and Aquila, a woman and a man, instruct the teacher Apollos.

Particularly in the Jewish world, but also in the Hellenistic, this would have been a striking novelty. The respect and legal protection accorded to women in the Old Testament may not be enough to be politically correct by modern standards. But, measured against the countries and civilizations around them, it stands out. Similarly, the leading role for women which is evident in the situation just outlined for the first generation of Christianity is unparalleled in the Greco-Roman world. Admittedly, in the generation after Luke's writing, when the pastoral letters to Timothy and Titus came to be written, the situation seems to have changed. There is less confidence, and women are relegated to a subordinate position. Luke shows us that it was not so in the first beginnings of the Christian community.

Jesus' confidence and freedom with regard to women was the beginning of a revolution. More than striking, indeed rather shocking, would have been the note that these women followed Jesus around to minister to him, leaving their own families and homesteads. One can imagine the scandal that this would have created. But Jesus is not afraid of public opinion.

Name-dropping

A STRIKING SIDELINE about Luke is his propensity for name-dropping. He is always keen to show that Christianity has a certain status. So here we are told that one of the women was wife to Herod's steward.

PRAYER

Lord, help me to grant equal respect to all people, men and women, rich and poor, whatever their status in society. Help me to remember that you created each one of us. Each one of us has infinite value in your eyes, and you love us as we are, with all our infuriating faults.

THE PARABLE OF THE SOWER

THE PARABLES ARE not always easy to understand because we lack their original context. The basic meaning of "parable" is "comparison," "image," or "riddle." Riddles and images can have different applications in different situations. Often the Gospel parables have come down to us without their original contexts, and without the original situation their exact force is often difficult to discern.

The Parable

THIS IS ONE of the great turning points in Jesus' ministry, when he turns away from the fickle crowds to instruct his chosen disciples. One can easily imagine him reflecting on the failure of his preaching with one group after another, but coming finally to dwell on the great fruitfulness of the few who did respond. He had tried one expedient after another, but all to no avail till he picked on the small group of the Twelve. So, in the short quotation from Isaiah which comes before the allegorical explanation, all receive the message, but some fail to understand. All are given the chance, but not all take it.

The Allegory

THE TEMPTATIONS THAT prevent the seed from bearing fruit are those we find throughout the Gospel. Firstly, the devil comes and takes away the seed. During Jesus' ministry the devil is significantly absent: At the end of the temptations in the desert the devil leaves him. No more is heard of the devil until Satan enters into Judas in Luke 22:3, and Jesus announces that now is the hour of darkness (22:53). The second failure of the seed is in those who lack perseverance and give up in time of temptation, for Luke is acutely aware of the pressures on Christians and the need for perseverance under persecution. Even their initial joy will not carry them through. The third failure is through those temptations and distractions that are stressed so often in this Gospel, especially wealth and luxury. Faith is not a momentary response, but demands generosity and perseverance over a long period, despite distractions and temptations.

The same is clear from Luke's alterations to the short parable of the lamp, which follows. The light of faith must shine brightly so that others may see it, not from the outside but "when they come in." It is to aid the understanding of those who believe. And instead of "Take notice of *what* you are hearing" (Mark), Luke concentrates on the mode of hearing and believing: "Take care *how* you listen"—just to hear the message is not enough.

The True Family of Jesus

THERE IS A subtle change in Luke here also. In Mark we find a sharp division between Jesus' family outside, and "the crowd sitting around him" inside. Jesus rather brushes off his family, indicating those around him as he says, "Here are my mother and brothers," in contradistinction from his own natural family. Such a separation is obviously unthinkable to Luke, after he has painted Mary's faith and response in such glowing colors at the annunciation and throughout the infancy narrative. So in Luke there is no separate group of family; they do not stand outside and send in a message, they continue to try to get to him. And Jesus responds with almost the same words but a different emphasis, praising them as the first examples of acceptance of the message, "My mother and my brothers are those who hear the word of God and put it into practice." Again Mary is the perfect example of the disciple, obedient and attentive to the will of God. This is reinforced by the change in position of the incident. It comes not as part of the hardening distinction between believers and unbelievers, but by being placed after the parable it makes Mary and the others the first hearers of the message of the parable, forerunners of all who accept and put into practice the message of Jesus.

PRAYER

Lord, keep me aware of the need to respond ever more deeply to your message, to grow in appreciation of it, despite the distractions and temptations of the world, and so to reach finally to full understanding of your revelation with you.

31

THE GERASENE DEMONIAC

THE LOCATION OF this miracle has caused plenty of trouble. The difficulty is that Gerasa is some eighteen miles southeast of the Lake of Galilee. Some versions of the Gospel avoid this difficulty by reading the place as "Gadara," whose territory reaches to within six miles of the Lake. The place name is not so important. The main point is that this seems to be Jesus' only visit to the Decapolis, the territory that lies to the southeast of the Lake of Galilee. This was not Jewish territory, but was marked by (and named after) ten fine Greek cities. Their remains still show a trace of their splendor, streets lined with noble colonnades, theaters ready for the classical Greek dramas, temples of Zeus, Diana, and the nymphs. The significance of the incident is that it is Jesus' only brush with the great Greco-Roman civilization that still marks our own culture. To this, too, he brings salvation and healing.

The main point of the story is the contrast between the pitiable state of the man in his deranged condition and the calm contentment as he sits at Jesus' feet. The folkloric element of the fate of the pigs is a visual flourish at the end of the story to underline the strength of the power that gripped the poor madman. The spirits beg not to be sent into the "Abyss," which is classical Greek language for the mythical abode of demons. They want to continue their mischievous and destructive reign above ground. Their return to the place of torment where they belong is a forceful demonstration of Jesus clearing evil and destruction from the world. On his one incursion into pagan territory, Jesus immediately makes inroads against the superstitions and idolatry of that culture.

The Gospel gives us an expressive picture of the poor victim. He is exiled from all civilization, living in the haunted abodes of the dead and not even properly dressed. His strength is daunting and uncontrollable, and as soon as he has broken his bonds he rushes off into the hideous desert, the eerie home of evil spirits. What makes it almost more tragic is that the attacks seem to have been periodic, presumably with periods of lucidity in between. It was only when the attacks came on that people would fetter him in an unsuccessful attempt to restrain him. But he always ended up in the wilds. Such periodic derangements to a friend whom one thinks one knows are easily ascribed to possession by a powerful and evil spirit alien to himself.

Salvation

LUKE SEES IN the miracle more than the merely physical or psychological significance of the cure. He characterizes the miracle as "how the man who had been possessed came to be *saved*" (v. 36), a phrase not present in the accounts of the other evangelists. This happens in other Lucan stories too, as in the following story of Jairus' daughter: "Only have faith and she will *be saved*" (v. 50). For Luke, Jesus is above all the Savior, as in the Old Testament God had been the Savior of Israel. By these subtle touches Luke reminds the reader that Jesus' work of healing, curing sickness, suffering, poverty, and misery is in fact a series of prophetic actions. The actions are important in themselves, but are also signs of something beyond themselves. Jesus' work is to save the total human being.

A further touching hint of Jesus' work and quality comes right at the end of the story: Jesus tells the man to go off home and report all that *God* had done for him. In fact he goes and proclaims all that *Jesus* had done for him. Are we to assume that Jesus is God, or just that he is doing God's work? In any case, this is already a strong hint, early in Jesus' ministry, of the divine quality of Jesus.

Discipleship

THIS SALVATION THAT Jesus brings turns the man into a full disciple. This is implied by his sitting at the feet of Jesus, a position of gratitude, obedience, and learning. Further, he also asks to stay with Jesus, and the disciples were originally chosen "to be with Jesus." Instead, he is sent off with the mission to spread the news of what God or Jesus has done for him, the first and only mission during Jesus' lifetime into this Greek region of the Decapolis.

PRAYER
Lord, you care for the whole person, everything about me. I can trust you with all my worries, for your one purpose is to save me.

THE WOMAN WITH A HEMORRHAGE, AND JAIRUS' DAUGHTER

STORIES ARE OFTEN interwoven in the Gospel. This shows up the significance of the two components by setting one off against the other. So Mark's account of the cleansing of the temple is set off on either side by the story of the cursing of the fig tree; the fig tree is the symbol of Israel, and so its cursing shows the barrenness of Israel, the meaning also of Jesus' prophetic action in the temple. The sending out of the disciples and their return is separated by the account of the death of John the Baptist; this emphasizes that preaching the gospel inevitably involves suffering and persecution. In the case of the two cures here, the story of the woman with a hemorrhage certainly increases the tension: And indeed, while Jesus is delayed by the woman with a hemorrhage, Jairus' daughter dies.

The story of Jairus' daughter is also linked, in one of the most remarkable of Luke's pairings, with the raising of the widow's son at Nain. There it is the male child of a female parent, here the female child of a male parent. Each is an only child, which makes the prospect of the loss all the more tragic for their parents. The crossover is another expression of the insistence in this Gospel on the equality of the two sexes before the Lord. The president of the synagogue was an important personage in the town. He ruled the synagogue, which was the center of religious life, and probably civic life too, in the village. There would be a board of elders, with a president elected for a fixed period. For such a man to be childless would be a tragedy indeed. For such a man to fall at Jesus' feet and do him reverence was an extreme token of putting trust in him. Luke underlines the sadness for Jairus, not only by telling us that his daughter was an only child, but also by stating at the beginning that she was only twelve years old. Mark mentions her age only at the end, when she has been cured and starts prancing around.

The woman with a hemorrhage is presumably suffering from a gynecological disorder. This disorder would not only have had its inherent difficulties, but would also have made her ritually unclean (according to the rules of Leviticus 15) and so forbidden to associate with normal society. Her desperate bid, amid the stiflingly close crowd, to touch simply the fringe of his cloak, would have incurred the utter disapproval of the religious authorities. It must have been a last resort; she had already spent all her money on unsuccessful treatment. To say that the cure changed her life is an understatement. (Mark makes the wry remark that medical treatment had in fact only made her worse. Luke omits this remark, and many have seen in this omission a confirmation of the tradition that the author of the Gospel was "my dear friend Luke, the doctor" mentioned by Paul in Colossians 4:14. He omitted the remark out of loyalty to the medical profession!)

Faith and Mission

THESE TWO MIRACLES are the last of four which immediately precede the mission of the disciples in 9:1, just as a series of four miracles immediately preceded the call of the disciples in 5:1. Both of these are demonstrations of the authority of Jesus in word and action. The same authority is seen in the ability to control the elements and heal as is seen in the teaching of Jesus and his chosen apostles.

In both these miraculous cures the faith of the recipients is underlined. In close proximity Jesus speaks to both his suppliants, first to the woman, "Your faith has saved you," then to the man, "Only have faith and she will be saved" (vv. 48, 50). In both cases the same open-ended word is used; she is or will be "saved." From her death, from her disability, or more totally? The one is a sign of the other. In the case of the little girl to be restored to life, and in the case of the older woman restored to normal life, these are potent signs of salvation of the whole person, the salvation Jesus came to bring to the world.

PRAYER

Lord, Jesus, as God made man you were alert to every human need of those around you, responding with love and generosity. Keep me aware that you are still present to us when we are in need, still protecting and cherishing us.

THE MISSION OF THE TWELVE

IT WAS A world where itinerant preachers were not unknown, and the instructions given by Jesus resemble those given to the wandering teachers of various popular philosophies, except that they are stricter. The task of these teachers is both more immediate, so that no distractions may enter in, and more powerful: Their needs will be supplied. No staff to lean on or to use for beating off stray dogs or animals. No money, which especially to Luke is a dangerous distraction. (It is interesting that Luke uses the word "silver" for "money," whereas Mark uses "copper"; Mark moves in a world where copper coins are common, whereas in Luke's world more expensive silver coinage is the norm.) No spare clothes or food. This is an ideal of poverty and reliance on the power of the task itself. There is a directness and confidence about this mission that is almost frightening; it brooks no compromise, allows no preparation, leaves room for no weakening. Preaching the kingdom is not an occupation for those who seek personal comfort and security. All this shows the nature and power of the kingdom that is being preached. It is a kingdom with authority: They are sent to preach and to heal—both works of authority—and that is what they do.

There is no compromise, either, in the reception of the message. If it is not received, the envoys are to employ the prophetic gesture of shaking the dust off their feet. This is a natural gesture of disgust and dissociation: "I will have nothing more to do with this place, getting rid of even the dust from the road." Luke is always keen to show fulfillment of prophecy. He shows us Paul and Barnabas doing just this when opposition is stirred up against them at Antioch and they are hustled out of the town.

A Renewal of Prophecy

IT WAS WIDELY accepted that prophecy had ceased in Israel. The great period of the prophets was before the exile. After the exile there had been one or two prophets, like Haggai and Zechariah, but now not for many hundreds of years. Now there was only a longing for the return of God's word, both for the guidance it would give and as a sign of God's affection for his people—however challenging and corrective this prophetic message had always been. The prophet Jeremiah was greatly revered as the champion of his people. A century and a half before Christ there was a tradition that Jeremiah would return as champion (2 Maccabees 15:11–14); a very similar story is told of Jeremiah protecting his own tomb during the 1948 Israeli War of Independence. There was a tradition also (Malachi 3:23) that Elijah would return "before the great and awesome Day of Yahweh comes." The Scrolls of Qumran, the fullest evidence we have for Jewish thought in Jesus' own century, show that the community on the desert shores of the Dead Sea were awaiting a prophet, "a voice crying in the desert."

All this testifies to a popular longing that God would return and speak to his people. It explains the immediate response to the Baptist and his message: He spoke into a void ready to receive his word. Even the temple authorities had to admit to themselves that his message had struck a chord with the people. Even the Jewish historian Josephus records that the Baptist was so influential that Herod took him into custody to prevent any possible uprising. The messengers could expect a response among the people, though perhaps durable results would be more difficult!

Herod the Fox

LATER IN LUKE (13:32) Jesus calls Herod "that fox." This Herod was the tetrarch of Galilee and other territory, though he did not inherit the full kingdom of his father, King Herod the Great. Jesus' name for him may stem from his activities in the Palestine area as a spy for the central Roman government. Luke does not want to bring the Baptist back into the picture by here telling the story of his execution by Herod, as Mark and Matthew do. Herod's curiosity here prepares for his reappearance in the story of the Passion. It also serves to put in a nutshell the amazement and wonder at this spreading movement.

PRAYER
Lord, give me the single-mindedness which you asked of your apostles. Let me enjoy what you give me, but not be distracted from concentration on the lasting values of your kingdom.

THE FEEDING OF THE FIVE THOUSAND

THE STORY OF the miraculous feeding must not be taken on its own in Luke. It is closely joined to the return of the apostles from their preaching journey, and to the short summary, at the beginning of the story, of more teaching and healing by Jesus. So it comes as the climax of these and sums up various themes that have been presented earlier in Luke's Gospel. Firstly, it must still be attached to the instructions given to the apostles as they set out on their journey, taking no food in their haversacks: It shows definitively that there is no need to fuss about provisions, for Jesus can provide food for his people, not merely for the apostles, but for vastly greater numbers. Secondly, it is the fulfillment of the beatitude "Blessed are those who are hungry now, for they shall be filled," which we see being accomplished in the ample food provided for the hungry crowds. Thirdly in this context, the disciples play an important part: It is the disciples rather than Jesus who act responsibly toward the crowds by taking pity on the multitudes. In Mark the crowds are "like sheep without a shepherd" and Jesus himself takes the initiative. In Luke, on the other hand, the Twelve have already begun to take responsibility for the people; they come up to Jesus and ask him to take action with regard to the hungry crowd; then, spurred on by him, they themselves sit the crowds down and distribute the food to them. This is in sharp contrast to the behavior of the disciples in Mark, where they reply to Jesus' command by some pretty sharp sarcasm; "Are we supposed to go and spend two hundred denarii on bread for them to eat?" Of this sarcasm there is no sign in Luke's account; now the disciples are willing, if puzzled, helpers. Thus Luke uses the narrative to express the theme of the kingdom and of the little band of disciples that is already beginning to develop in so many ways.

The Miracle of Feeding

THE MEANING OF the miracle in its original version in Mark was that Jesus was shown to be the messianic shepherd feeding his sheep, as in the psalm, on pastures green. He was also acting as the prophet Elisha had acted. The story has not lost this meaning in Luke. The prophet Elisha provided bread for his followers in the desert, just as Moses had done for his people. The process of the narrative is so similar to the Elisha account in 2 Kings 4:42–44 that there can be no doubt that the evangelist intends to show that Jesus is acting in just the same way as Elisha. There is the same process of dialogue, the same distribution, the same plenty, the same satisfaction, and the same leftovers. Only, the miracle done by Jesus is many times greater, for Elisha feeds one hundred men with ten loaves, while Jesus feeds five thousand with five loaves. Jesus is thus seen to be acting in the line of the prophets, but also to be the greatest of the prophets, greater even than Moses.

A Messianic Celebration

THE PLENTY PROVIDED ("they all ate as much as they wanted"), and again demonstrated by the abundance of scraps left over, is a sign of the plenty of the messianic banquet. The number of twelve, featuring in the group of the Twelve and the twelve baskets of scraps, suggests that Jesus' community is the new Israel, corresponding to the twelve tribes of ancient Israel. The Twelve represent the foundation stones of the new Israel. The whole scene, therefore, shows in many ways the feast of the Messiah with his new people of God, which has come to fruition at the end of time.

When it comes to the blessing and distribution of the food, we are reminded of the meal at the Last Supper, when Jesus again, with his disciples around him, took bread, said the blessing, broke the bread, and handed it to his disciples. The feeding near Bethsaida is, then, also a foretaste of the eucharistic celebration.

PRAYER
Lord, your delight is to be with your disciples at the eucharistic meal. Grant that I may there welcome you into my heart with the overflowing joy of your generosity, eager to be your willing disciple, zealous to do your work.

THE FIRST PROPHECY OF THE PASSION

ON THE WHOLE, Luke has been following the order of incidents in Mark's
Gospel. Now he does something quite remarkable, cutting out a considerable number of incidents, given in Mark 6:48–8:26. This is either because
he thinks them unnecessary or uninteresting to his audience, or because
he wants to press on to use this scene as part of his developing picture of
the disciples.

The growing understanding of the disciples reaches a new stage with
the confession of Peter that Jesus is the Christ of God, or God's Messiah.
Till then we have had a series of hints laid down that Jesus is a prophet,
and a series of questions raised. The demons have acknowledged Jesus as
Son of God, but human beings have simply been puzzled, astonished, and
awestruck at his miracles and his teaching, as Simon and his companions
in the boat, as the people of the territory of the Gerasenes, as Jairus and
his wife were. People have asked, "Who is this man, that even forgives
sins . . . that gives orders even to winds and waves and they obey him?"
Jesus has been repeatedly greeted as a prophet. He has himself given the
meaning of his miracles to the envoys from John the Baptist as fulfilling
the messianic prophecies of Isaiah; he has sent his followers out on a
messianic mission; on their return he has provided food for them and
others, just as Elisha had done.

Now, in response to Jesus' questioning, the other disciples tentatively
put forward the opinions of others that Jesus is various of the ancient
prophets. For centuries there had been a dearth of prophecy. Although the
message of the prophets was normally critical of society and often uncomfortable, the Jews felt acutely that these messengers of God were a sign of
God's love for them—like the guidance or even the scolding of a loving
parent. So they felt the silence of prophecy and longed for its renewal. So
clearly many hoped that Jesus was at least the renewal of prophecy. But
Peter goes further and comes straight to the mark with "the Christ of
God." At the time of Jesus this could have many shades of meaning, a

warlike leader who would liberate Israel from the Romans, a king, an anointed priest. At the very least it is God's chosen messenger who is to bring God's will to fulfillment at the end of time. By his actions and his teaching, Jesus has been showing what this means. Now, in reply to Peter's declaration, he begins to show that it must mean suffering also.

Discipleship and Persecution

A STRIKING DIFFERENCE from Mark's account, which must be deliberate on Luke's part, is that there is no mention of failure on the part of the disciples. In Mark's account, Peter rejects out of hand any idea of Jesus suffering, and is sternly rebuked, "Get behind me, Satan." At each of the three prophecies of the Passion in Mark, the disciples misunderstand or reject the idea of suffering, and have to be told forcefully by Jesus that any followers of his must share his sufferings. In Luke, the solidarity between Jesus and his followers is considerably stronger. There is taking place, so to speak, a crescendo of bonding between Jesus and his followers. Not only is there no objection from Peter, and so no rebuke to him. Also the need to share in Christ's suffering is addressed not merely to the chosen group of disciples, but to all disciples, future as well as present: "Speaking to all, he said . . ." Luke has in mind a lesson not just for the Twelve but for all who will set out to follow Jesus. He stresses that it is not a one-off event that is in view, but the daily challenge of discipleship, by adding "take up the cross *daily.*"

It is often questioned whether the expression "take up the cross" can stem from Jesus. Could he have used the expression before his own crucifixion? The ugly sight of crucified bodies rotting on gibbets by the roadside, and the process of dragging the execution beam to the place of execution, can hardly have been unknown. But the expression clearly takes on massive added significance after Jesus' death and resurrection.

PRAYER

Grant me, Lord, to join more fully with you in your sufferings. Help me to realize the privilege of joining you in your passion, through the crosses you send to me in daily life, both great and small.

THE TRANSFIGURATION

THE STORY OF the transfiguration of Jesus is knit into Luke's developing narrative. It comes as a climax of the process we have seen developing as the disciples understand more and more who and what Jesus is. This experience of Jesus transfigured comes as a high point of this understanding. It is also the continuation and development of the message of the approaching suffering and Passion of Jesus, which is just beginning to impinge on the consciousness of the disciples: The three figures speak together "of his passing which he was to accomplish in Jerusalem."

One important element in the scene is that it starts with an ascent of "the mountain" to pray. We have no means of knowing which mountain, though Christian tradition has localized the scene at Mount Tabor, an awesome, rounded mountain rising isolated from the fertile Galilean plain. The important thing is that a mountain is the favored place for an encounter with God. Just as the first prophecy of the Passion, a few verses previously, had emerged from Jesus' prayer ("He was praying alone, and his disciples came to him . . ."), so at the transfiguration he is praying. Luke is insistent that the knowledge of God and of his will must be founded on prayer. There is no approach to God without first yielding oneself to God in prayer.

The imagery and symbolism of this experience of Jesus, before he begins his journey up to Jerusalem and to the Passion, is rich with Old Testament allusions. His sparkling white clothing can mean only that he is seen as a heavenly being. The support of Moses and Elijah is difficult to evaluate, for it can have many overtones. Perhaps Moses and Elijah stand respectively for the Law and the prophets of the Old Testament. Perhaps they are figures who were expected to return at the end of time, for Jesus is frequently represented both as a second Moses and as an Elijah figure. Alternatively, they may be being presented as prophets who themselves received an experience of God on mountains, namely Sinai and Horeb respectively.

The climax of the experience is, however, of the glory of God. The vision of the three heavenly figures is bathed in the glory of God, which persists as a sort of afterglow in the glory of Jesus when the disciples rouse themselves. It has a fascination and a terror, so that Peter says, "It is wonderful to be here," and yet as they enter into the cloud (another symbol and expression of God's glory) they are rightly afraid. It is a reminiscence of the glory of Yahweh which was shown to Moses on Mount Sinai, a terrifying, awesome experience, the nearest a human being can get to experiencing God, "whom no man can see and live." The vision of God in the temple reduced even Isaiah to quaking, terrified awareness of his own sinfulness, so that "the Holy One of Israel" remained his slogan and inspiration throughout his message. Peter's strange and baffled suggestion that they should make three shelters is perhaps an idea that they should make three shrines so that the experience might remain permanent.

This climax of this awesome experience of God is the divine voice confirming the authority of Jesus as God's chosen messenger. To contemporaries this would have been clearer still, for there are other contemporary stories of a voice from heaven that confirms the authority of a teacher, underpinning his message with God's own authority. Further, Luke already has his eye on the proclamation of the gospel message when he carefully says, "The disciples kept silence and *at that time* told no one what they had seen." There is a direct line between the message of God, the message of the disciples, and the reception of the gospel.

Thus the disciples are strengthened at the beginning of the preparation for the final prophetic act of the journey up to Jerusalem and the Passion.

PRAYER

Lord, grant me devotion in prayer, grant me even to glimpse your glory and to long for the full vision of your presence. May I be inspired particularly at moments of trial at least by the knowledge that your glory is there, infinitely superior to any human power, and even to the power of my own sinfulness and incompetence.

The Disciples' Failure

It is staggering and yet obviously deliberate that now, immediately after this vision of divine glory that was the transfiguration, the weakness and incomprehension of the disciples should be drummed in by a series of incidents. These form a whole group between the transfiguration and the beginning of the journey to Jerusalem. Luke seems to have welded together into one unit several incidents, the scene of the epileptic child, the second prophecy of the Passion, and finally, the dispute about greatness.

The incomprehension of the disciples is a striking feature of the Gospel. In the first half of the Gospel, leading up to the eventual confession of Peter at Caesarea Philippi, they are several times rebuked by Jesus for their slowness to understand, and are even reproached for "hardness of heart," like the Pharisees themselves. On more than one occasion they treat Jesus to quite unpleasant doses of sarcasm. When Peter has finally recognized that Jesus is the Christ, they still cannot stomach the idea that he is a suffering Messiah. Every time he foretells the Passion, they show their incomprehension by turning a deaf ear to his lessons on the ministry of service and by squabbling about their own precedence in the kingdom.

On the whole, Luke softens this criticism of the disciples, and stresses their close companionship with Jesus and their responsiveness to him. This was especially clear, as we have seen, in the leading up to the transfiguration. But now their failure to share with Jesus comes through with all the more force.

The Epileptic Boy

Despite having been given earlier the power over all evil spirits, the disciples now fail to drive out the spirit that is tormenting the young man. In this context it must be the disciples who are envisaged in Jesus' exasperated rebuke to the "faithless and perverse generation." The inability of the chosen disciples to help contrasts unfavorably with the obviously heartfelt prayers of the boy's father. Luke increases the father's plight by pointing out that the sufferer is an only son. The contrast between the failure of the disciples and Jesus' power is made all the more striking by the effortless way in which Jesus triumphs over the spirit of epilepsy. There is none of the graphic description of struggle as given in Mark's account, nor of the father's desperate faith: "I believe; help my unbelief!" (Mark 9:24, RSV). Jesus restores the boy by his simple overriding authority. It is all over in a flash, and the crowds are left goggling at the greatness of God. At the end of the passage the ineptitude of the disciples is again underlined by the fact that others are succeeding in driving out evil spirits in Jesus' name, while the disciples both fail to do this themselves and attempt to prevent others from doing it. Is it that they lack faith? Or is it that they are too preoccupied with their own position and status, as the dispute in verse 46 suggests?

The Second Prophecy of the Passion Neglected

THE DISCIPLES AGAIN show their insensitivity by completely disregarding Jesus' prophecy of his approaching suffering. Throughout this journey up to Jerusalem he clearly has the coming Passion in mind. So much was made clear by the discussion about his "passing" during the scene of the transfiguration. It breaks the surface again in the three prophecies of the Passion and in such remarks as "It would not be right for a prophet to die outside Jerusalem" (13:33). This is enough to show that the prospect of his fate and its inevitability was constantly before his mind. Yet all this the disciples fail to understand. Instead of asking what it means, they seem to turn away and block it out of their minds. Instead, they immediately begin to argue about their own positions, till Jesus gives them a counterdemonstration by means of the little child. Children are not really any more innocent or straightforward than adults—only less experienced and so less skilled in deception. Perhaps the quality Jesus puts forward is, rather, dependence and willingness to receive. Whatever it is, the disciples have a lot to learn on the road up to Jerusalem.

PRAYER
Lord, you have chosen me to be your follower and disciple. Often I fail to understand your ways and close my ears to your message. Make me more sensitive to your guidance and responsive to your will.

JOURNEY TO JERUSALEM

NOW BEGINS THE great journey to Jerusalem, full of presage and omen for the Passion of Jesus, full of presage also for the resurrection and the worldwide mission of the apostles that will result from it. Jerusalem is, for Luke, the hinge: There Jesus dies and is raised, from there the word spreads to the ends of the earth. So Luke deserts the Marcan structure he has followed in at least close outline since the baptism of Jesus. He rearranges the material and brings in more from other sources, focusing the whole on the goal of Jerusalem. All other distracting geographical references are suppressed, so that the reader is not diverted from the intention of Jesus who now "resolutely turned his face toward Jerusalem."

The Old Testament atmosphere and regular reference to the prophets again and again remind us that Jesus is fulfilling the whole movement of the Old Testament. The journey is put under the sign of Jesus being "taken up." Superficially this may mean only his "going up" to Jerusalem. But on a deeper level a hint is already being given of the ascension, when Jesus will be "taken up" into heaven. This in its turn already reminds us of Elijah, who was taken up into heaven at his death, and perhaps also of Moses, who was last seen before his death on Mount Nebo, and whose tomb was unknown. The Gospel of John gives a still fuller meaning to this "being taken up," regarding the "lifting up" of Jesus onto the cross as his exaltation or lifting up to heaven, where he would draw all people to himself and also come to share in the heavenly glory of the Father; the lifting up is interpreted as the glorification of Jesus.

The Apostolic Journey

ANOTHER REMINDER OF Moses is the appointment of the "seventy-two others" whom Jesus sends out ahead of him. In just the same way Moses had appointed seventy-two elders to assist him in his task. The background of traveling is surely significant in all this. For Luke, traveling is a way of life. The people of Moses were on the move for forty years in the desert, and similarly the apostle of Jesus is always on the move. According to one calculation, Paul traveled ten thousand miles in the course of his mission, an extraordinary feat of endurance in a world where ten miles a day by road was a dusty and exhausting average. Luke, too, must have been acutely conscious of traveling from his own journeys in the apostolic cause. This is why traveling is the background of so much of his double volume.

A Sign of Contradiction

THERE ARE NO illusions that the journey is easy or has a happy outcome. Some scholars have seen a balancing pattern in all the incidents of the trip, by which (like onion skins progressively peeled off) the first balances the last, the second balances the penultimate, the third balances the ante-penultimate, and so on. How general this pattern is may be doubted, but at least the first and last incidents balance each other. Each of them is a rejection: At the beginning Jesus is rejected by the Samaritans (and the suggestion of calling down fire from heaven again reminds us of Elijah calling down fire from heaven on those who come to arrest him in 2 Kings 1). At the end, Jesus is rejected in Jerusalem, so the first rejection provides a sort of premonition at the start of the trip that has its fulfillment at the end.

Much of the teaching on this journey—and the material on the journey is overwhelmingly sayings of Jesus rather than actions—is about discipleship. Accordingly, it starts with three stern sayings on the demands of being a disciple of Jesus, as though to say, "Let there be no illusions: You are entering on a tough course." The fact that none of them records any reply shows that the evangelist is more interested in the saying than in any story in which it occurred; the lesson is general, not limited to any particular person. The first demands total homelessness. The second puts the claims of the kingdom above the most sacred of human ties. The third requires ceaseless and concentrated dedication: If you lose concentration for a moment with a handplow, the whole endeavor goes to pieces.

PRAYER

Give me strength, Lord, to follow you on your journey, even though it is a hard road. Give me your company and your inspiration on the way.

THE MISSION OF THE SEVENTY-TWO

THE FIRST QUESTION is why Luke gives us a second account of mission, when 9:1–6 has already given the instructions to the Twelve for their mission. Luke seems to dislike doublets (this may be why he omits the second miraculous feeding of the four thousand after the five thousand, and the walking on the water after the calming of the storm), but he does not mind repeating really important teaching. After all, he tells the story of the conversion of Paul three times in the Acts, and—as here—with some slight variations for elegance and to avoid boredom. The differences are probably more for literary variation than for theological significance: On the first mission they are forbidden staff and bread, on the second they are forbidden sandals and greetings on the way. The same message of urgency and single-mindedness lies behind both.

The answer to a second question also throws light on the first: Is it seventy or seventy-two disciples? The original Greek text is hard to establish; some manuscripts give seventy, some seventy-two, and it is difficult to decide between them. There is an important parallel to this in the Old Testament. In Genesis 10 the nations of the earth are enumerated. In the Hebrew text there are seventy of them, in the Greek, seventy-two. When Moses chose the elders to help him, there were also seventy, and by tradition these were one for each nation of the world. Whatever the solution to the numerical problem, the importance of this muddle is that it suggests that Luke had in mind the mission of the apostles to all the nations of the world, sent out two by two, but nevertheless one for each nation.

Then the two missions make sense, the Twelve being sent in chapter 9 to the tribes of Israel, and the Seventy(-two) sent in chapter 10 to the non-Jewish nations. The same two-stage mission comes again in the parable of the great feast, where the messengers are sent first to the outcasts within the city (that is, Israel), and then to those outside the city (the Gentiles). This is also, of course, the pattern of Luke's two volumes, the first describing the message to Israel, the second (the Acts of the Apostles) that to the nations. On this wider mission perhaps the most notable variation is the threat of danger and rejection.

A Gospel of Peace

THE FIRST WORDS of the missioners are to be "Peace be to this house," and they are to bring peace to those who will receive it. This is more than the conventional Jewish greeting (still used today), *Shalom.* Luke sees the gospel importantly as "the good news of peace," as Peter announces to Cornelius and his household in Acts. Right from the beginning of the Gospel the angels at the nativity sing, "On earth peace" and Zechariah's canticle starts "Now, Master, you are letting your servant go in peace" when he has received the child Jesus. The sinful woman who weeps on Jesus' feet is told to "go in peace" with her sins forgiven. The Gospel of John will give this concept an even greater depth, for the peace of Christ is part of the indwelling of Christ in his followers: "My peace I bequeath to you, my peace I give you." Peace is the final blessing of Jesus in the discourses at the Last Supper, and again his greeting to them in the upper room after the resurrection. In a world of unrest, turbulence, malice, and aggression, the Christian gift of peace is beyond value. So each of Paul's letters begins with the greeting of "Peace" and many of them end with it too. Peace must be founded on respect for others and their needs, avoiding the temptation to domineer or insist on one's own interests.

The Cities of the Lakeside

IT IS IN contrast to this offer of peace that the fate of the lakeside cities is so daunting. The words of the curse, "Did you want to be raised high as heaven? You shall be flung down to hell" are an allusion to the fate of proud Babylon in Isaiah 14. The city that aspired to rule the world, like Lucifer, would, for its pride, be consigned to the lowest depths.

PRAYER

Lord, as your apostles were the agents of peace, let me, too, bring your peace to others. Take from me all worry and insecurity, in the knowledge that if I trust in you rather than my own strength, you will give me your own peace to abide with me forever.

A FINAL BLESSING

THIS LONG SECTION on disciples and discipleship ends with a double blessing: Jesus blesses his Father in gratitude, and his disciples for the revelation that has been given to them, and which they are to spread to others. Between these two blessings he pronounces one of the deepest reflections in the Synoptic Gospels on the relationship between Father and Son.

The Eagerness of Children

THE BLESSING BEGINS with Luke's characteristic theme of reversal. Mary's hymn of praise in the *Magnificat* centered on gratitude that God had "pulled down princes from their thrones and raised high the lowly." The beatitudes promise the kingdom of God to those who are poor now, and laughter to those who weep now. Now the reversal concerns revelation: It is not the learned and clever who receive the secrets of revelation but "mere children." This comes close to Paul's insistence, writing to the Corinthians, that God's folly is wiser than human wisdom, that human wisdom was unable to recognize God, and "it was God's own pleasure to save believers through the folly of the gospel" (1 Corinthians 1:21).

The preference for children is no romantic idealization of childhood, about their supposed innocence or guilelessness; rather, it gives the clue to why Jesus earlier set a child among the disciples as a model. One real universal characteristic of children is willingness to learn, an appreciation that they are an empty canvas on which there is still much to be drawn. Imitation is a feature of childhood from the very beginning. Adults hate being corrected; for children it is an inevitable part of life, and something on which to grow. The eagerness to grow in mind is as keen as the longing to grow in body, and a child realizes that while it can do nothing to speed bodily growth, it can do much to speed mental development. It is this eagerness to receive and to learn that Jesus here praises as the prerequisite of revelation.

The "Johannine Thunderbolt"

BETWEEN THE TWO blessings at beginning and end of this little section comes the stunning statement about the relationship of the Son to the Father. Nothing else like it exists in the Synoptic Gospels, but it is amply filled out in the Gospel of John. The basic theology is that of the "shaliah." This is a Hebrew term in rabbinic writings for an envoy, sent with specific powers. The envoy is regarded as having the same powers, deserving the same respect, holding the same position as his principal. He is sent out by and reports back to the principal. In his turn he can appoint envoys to extend his work. This is clearly the concept that stands behind much of John's expression of the relationship of the Son to the Father, who shows him everything he himself does, who gives all judgment to the Son: "As the Father has life in himself, so he has granted the Son also to have life in himself" (John 5:26).

The importance of this statement comes from the fact that the Hebrew mind defines in dynamic rather than static terms. The later Trinitarian theological definitions of the great Councils are given in static terms. That is, instead of describing the relationship of Son to Father in the Greek terms of essence and nature, as did the early Church Councils (dominated by Greek thought), the Hebrew mind describes in terms of powers and action what a person does rather than what a person is. So here the Son reveals the Father, and to know the Son is to know the Father. Just as in John, judgment has been entrusted to the Son, so here "everything" has been entrusted to the Son, so that the Son is the plenipotentiary of the Father, and stands in the place of the Father.

PRAYER

Father, you reveal yourself to us in your Son. Teach me to pray and meditate over this revelation you give, and draw me ever closer into company with your Son and so with you.

41   <u>LUKE 10:25-37</u>

THE GOOD SAMARITAN

The Great Commandment

THIS LITTLE DIALOGUE is the only scene where Luke on his own gives the classic form of Jesus dialogue, common in Mark, and possibly remembered as typical of Jesus' own challenging method of teaching. It happens in four moves. Someone comes up and asks Jesus a question. Jesus does not answer but replies with his own question. The original questioner gives an answer, usually unsatisfactory (but here wholly satisfactory). Lastly, Jesus gives his own solution.

There is a fascinating difference in Luke's account from Mark's. In Mark, the questioner asks which is the first commandment, and Jesus gives the reply. There could never really be any doubt about which was the first commandment of the Law. It was incorporated into the great monotheistic creed of Israel in Deuteronomy 6:4–5, which every faithful Jew still recites in the daily prayer: "Yahweh our God is the one, the only Yahweh. You must love Yahweh your God with all your heart, with all your soul, with all your strength." In Mark, the punch of Jesus' answer is that he adds, unasked, the second commandment of love of neighbor. This is typical of Jesus: He was always going deeper than the questioner wanted him to, and making fuller demands than were expected! This happens also with the tribute coin: "Pay Caesar what belongs to Caesar (that is harmless enough), *and God what belongs to God.*

In Luke's account the two are joined together, and the speaker is the lawyer. He is duly praised by Jesus, but then nearly spoils things by his blustering question, "anxious to justify himself"; with one deft touch of pompous bluster Luke brings the lawyer to life! On the other hand, the whole dialogue is neatly sewn together by the idea of "life" at beginning and end: "What must I do to inherit eternal life? . . . Do this and life is yours." This is one of only two occasions in Luke when the concept of eternal life appears—the other being the story of the rich aristocrat who comes to Jesus with the same question. In John the concept is frequent, and sums up all the benefits brought by Jesus, much the same as the concept of the kingship of God.

The Parable

LUKE ADDS ONE of his well-loved stories. The old path from Jerusalem to Jericho runs down the Wadi Qilt, a deep, twisting canyon with rocky sides and blistering heat, some four hours' fast walk. Today you can round a corner and find yourself in the middle of a flock of goats, herded by a bedouin boy and his noisy dogs. Just as easily it could be the bandits of Jesus' tale. There is a certain wit about the story: The priest and Levite are in a nasty moral dilemma. They could not miss seeing the traveler, even by passing by "on the other side": The bottom of the canyon is never more than just over sixty feet wide. It is not simply that they pass by unfeelingly. If the huddled victim of the bandits turns out to be dead, they could be defiled by contact with a corpse and disqualified from their sacred duties (and deprived of the income from them!).

The hero of the story turns out to be the Samaritan. It is the first time (apart from a brief mention in 9:52) we have come across that people whom the Jews disliked so much. They were descended from an amalgam of peoples deported by the Assyrians, centuries earlier, to the territory north of Judea. They were near enough to the Jews, both territorially and in religion, to be felt as a threat, with all the dislike engendered by rivalry. Yet Christianity spread to them early enough, and Jesus himself unforgettably drew the Samaritan woman at Jacob's well to be his follower. For Luke they are therefore the paradigm of the foreigners who are invited by the call of Jesus to share the privileges of the Jews. To counter the exclusiveness of the Jews, Luke shows the Samaritans being more responsive than the Jews to the message of Jesus. The traveler shows open-hearted generosity at a chance meeting with a total stranger.

So here the Samaritan fulfills the commandment of love that the two Jews neglect. There is one of those little logical knots we have occasionally encountered in Luke: The story is supposed to show who is my neighbor to whom I should show love. Instead, it illustrates who the neighbor is who shows love to me.

PRAYER

Lord, you call on me to show the same love to all as you yourself show. Make me open-hearted and generous to those in need, help me to see them all as my own brothers and sisters.

MARTHA AND MARY

GEOGRAPHICALLY, MARTHA AND Mary have no right to appear here. According to John's Gospel, they belong in Bethany, less than half an hour's walk from Jerusalem, where they lived with their brother Lazarus. In Luke the great journey up to Jerusalem has hardly begun. But one of the features of the journey is that Luke suppresses geographical details that would distract from the sense of going up to the Passion. Geography is not his principle of arrangement, and perhaps the story comes here as part of a series on hospitality (in which it fits with the story of the good Samaritan), particularly hospitality to those who bring God's message (in which it fits well after the instructions to and mission of the disciples).

The story is told with the liveliness typical of the characterization in Luke's parables, Mary's tranquil composure vividly contrasting with Martha's busy fussiness. It is so typical of the activist, who likes to fill every available moment and would be miserable at having nothing to do, to complain of lack of help. Not content with fussing around, Martha is obviously the type who blurts out everything, even family secrets, even in front of important guests. They were not children, and must have lived together for some years, so Mary's behavior can have come as no surprise to Martha—yet still she scolds her, or, rather, even asks the guest to scold her. One does not have the impression of a happy household if the sibling rivalry was such that Martha needed to go about correcting her sister through a third party! There is surely a deliberate contrast in the manner of speech between Martha, who does not even have the courtesy or warmth to name her sister, and Jesus, who softens his correction by affectionately using her name twice, "Martha, Martha."

Jesus' reply is typical also of Luke's emphasis on detachment from possessions. There is no need for them, and the one thing necessary is to listen to the Lord. So much has been clear since the annunciation stories, and especially since the presentation of Mary and the disciples as the ones who listen. At the base of this is the simple lesson of human courtesy in hospitality: The personality of the guest is more important than any entertainment, and attention to the guest is the prime compliment to be paid. When the guest is a teacher, this is even more obviously the case.

Contemplation and Action

IN CHRISTIAN ASCETICAL tradition the two sisters have become the symbols of the contemplative and active life, the lives centered respectively on prayer and on translating prayer into action. This builds on the assumption that the parable is contrasting two ways of prayer; in fact, it would be more accurate to see it as contrasting two ways of attentiveness. Luke does not suggest that Martha's service is wrong. To begin with, he uses the same word for her service as that used for the service of the Seven who are appointed to serve the poor of the faithful in the early community ideally described in Acts. Furthermore, when the Greek literally has "Mary has chosen the *good* part," this does not imply that Martha's part is bad. It is simply that comparatives ("better," "worse," etc.) are rare in Gospel Greek. Jesus' language was stark and uncompromising.

There may be another dimension to the story. The answer to the lawyer's question about eternal life (at the beginning of the previous section) was the double commandment, love of God and love of neighbor. The command to love one's neighbor as oneself was illustrated by the story of the good Samaritan. Now the command to love God above all things is illustrated by the story of Martha and Mary. Jesus is not only addressed as "Lord!," which happens in Mark, and may mean no more than "Sir!" He is also described (v. 41) as "*the* Lord," which strongly suggests the Lord God. So Mary's love of Jesus is an illustration of love of God with the whole heart.

PRAYER
Lord, let me listen to your word. Do not let your message be
clouded over or crowded out by my own preoccupations and busy-ness.
Give me the tranquillity and openness to hear your message in my
head and in my heart.

THE LORD'S PRAYER

THIS IS THE first of three short sections in a collection of teachings on how Jesus' disciples should pray. But it is prefaced by the notice that Jesus was praying when his disciples came asking him to teach them how to pray. Here again, as often in Luke, Jesus is at prayer, which was the wellspring of his being and his activity, and here again Jesus is the model for the disciples, teaching them to pray as he himself prays. The followers of Jesus imitate him in his prayer, his miracles, his suffering, and his passion.

Luke's version of the Lord's Prayer is simpler than the more familiar version taken from Matthew's Gospel. The first striking difference is the stark "Father!" with which it opens. Matthew's "Our Father in heaven" is more courtly and more Jewish. Luke's version has the directness and immediacy of Jesus' own prayer in the Garden and elsewhere, in which he addressed God warmly and simply as "Father." This "Abba" became so treasured among Christians that the Aramaic phrase was retained as a sort of talisman even in the Greek letters of Paul. It must have been regarded as the guarantee and reassurance that Christians could use this address as adopted children to their Father.

The Coming of the Kingdom

IN LUKE'S VERSION there are only two petitions in the first part of the prayer, concerned with God. Luke omits Matthew's third petition, "May your will be done." Perhaps he thought it was adequately voiced in the two prayers he does have. There are other occasions also when he omits references to God's will when they occur in Matthew's Gospel.

Luke's first petition is identical with that of Matthew, "May your name be held holy." It is a prayer that the holiness of God may be recognized. It must remind one of the call of the prophet Isaiah in Isaiah 6, when he saw the Lord enthroned in the temple, his train a sort of cloud of smoke, filling the sanctuary. So awesome was this vision that even the seraphs covered their faces to cry, "Holy, holy, holy!" Isaiah's reaction is terror and awareness of his own and the people's sinfulness, needing to be cleansed by fire before he can announce the Lord's message. Henceforth he will always call God "the Holy One of Israel." No human being can stand before God; it is this holiness and total otherness from all creation that must be recognized.

The second petition, "May your kingdom come," touches the heart of Jesus' message. It cannot be described shortly, for it sums up the whole of his activity. He brought the kingdom (or perhaps better, the kingship) of God by the prophetic actions of his miracles of healing and forgiveness, by his teaching and the response in human hearts, by the loving obedience to his Father on the cross in which his whole life was crystallized. Yet in another sense Jesus' activity on earth was only the beginning of the establishment of the kingship of God, and we can still pray that God's kingship be fully accomplished. It is all too clear that the evils of malice, suffering, pain, and death continue in the world, and God's kingship is not fully realized till all these have been abolished. The vision of the return to paradise is far from fulfillment.

Human Needs

THE SECOND SET of petitions is concerned with human needs. Again Luke's version is more direct: He omits the final "but save us from evil (or the Evil One)." The first of these three petitions is concerned with humdrum human needs. Luke makes the request more insistent than Matthew's calmer version, so that it should be translated literally, *"Go on giving us our bread every day."* Just so, Luke insists that the Christian must take up the cross every single day. Of course, "bread" stands in biblical language for food in general, not necessarily the produce of wheat. It is equally applicable to pasta, rice, or salsa!

The next petition is the dangerous one. We blandly and unthinkingly say (in Matthew's version) "Forgive us . . . as we have forgiven." Can we really be easy in our minds at asking God to mete out to us no more than the forgiveness we mete out to others? Luke challenges the follower of Christ to assert boldly, "For we ourselves forgive each one who is in debt to us." Do we?

PRAYER

Father, may your kingdom come. Forgive us our sins, whatever they are.

A Parable on Prayer

The Selfish Householder

THIS IS ANOTHER of Luke's lively parables with his brilliant characterization. Luke does not insist on allegory. If it were an allegory, the householder would stand in the place of God. In an allegory, such as the parable of the sower or (in Matthew's Gospel) the wheat and the tares, each element in the story has a corresponding element in the meaning. For an allegory, a sort of key can be provided, as it is in the case of those two parables, explaining the correspondences. Not every parable is an allegory; sometimes, as here or in the parable of the dishonest steward, there is just one point of comparison.

In any case, Luke is not afraid to make the householder act—like most of us—from mixed motives. His characters often do the right thing for the wrong reasons. Like most of us, they are mixed characters, neither plaster-cast saints nor utter blackguards. The scenario for this story is a small village and a one-room house. The master of the house sleeps in the inner recesses, farthest from the door. If he is to get up and answer the door, he will have to climb over his sleeping children, stretched out over the rest of the floor. So he makes the sleeping children his excuse. However, the battering on the door persists, and in the end, rather than be shamed by the whole village being woken up and hearing of his refusal to offer hospitality, he climbs over the children and gives the traveler whatever he wants (a hint of desperation or exasperation, not just "what he wants," but "whatever he wants"!). There are other occasions in the parables when shame is a motive for action: The crafty steward would be "too ashamed" to beg. Human respect is often a powerful motive in our lives, and one of the encouraging aspects about the parables in Luke is how like ourselves the characters are: They often do the right thing from mixed motives!

One may question the origin of this short, isolated parable, which comes in no other Gospel. Luke is a master storyteller (was this the reason his community commissioned him to write the Gospel?), and can turn

Matthew's stiff contrast of the two sons into the vibrant tale of the prodigal son, or a single remark in the book of Proverbs into the parable of the unjust judge. Perhaps this story of the selfish householder is no more than an expansion of the sayings that follow it.

Effective Prayer

THERE FOLLOW THREE little sayings which Luke shares with Matthew. All three are imperatives, followed by the result. To express the result, the "theological passive" is used. The Jews, out of reverence, avoided using the name of God. At this time the sacred personal name of God, YHWH, was held too sacred ever to be pronounced, and "Adonai" or "Lord" was used in its stead. In present-day Judaism this too is avoided, and "the Name" is substituted in its place. But one way of avoiding even that is to use the passive. What is here meant, then, is "Ask, and God will provide. Knock, and God will open the door."

This brings us starkly up against the problem of our unanswered prayer. The Father may not give a snake instead of a fish or a scorpion instead of an egg, but he certainly does not always give the fish or the egg! Again, it is important that the parable of the selfish householder is not an allegory. The householder gives the traveler whatever he demands; God does not. It is possible only to suggest the beginning of an answer. It is like a human father and his children. The Father knows best, and the child trusting in his love can only yield to that love and wisdom of the Father. We cannot understand the wisdom of God. Like Job, we cannot demand an explanation. We can only ask and trust. The battering on the door is only a sign and expression of our trust that the householder will not leave us benighted.

PRAYER

Lord, you give us your Holy Spirit as your best gift, the Spirit of love and trust. You know our needs and you know how best they can be fulfilled. I know that you will not give me a scorpion, but do sometimes give me the egg for which I ask!

45   LUKE 11:14–28

REACTIONS TO JESUS

Jesus and Beelzebul

HOW DOES THIS controversy get here? In Mark it comes much earlier in the Gospel (Mark 3:22–27), forming the boundary between Jesus' teaching to the crowds and his turning to instruct the disciples. Luke's change of position for the episode makes two important points. First, it shows that Luke is concerned in this section to show different reactions to the message of Jesus; all the incidents form a study of the various ways in which Jesus' message can be accepted or rejected. Second, the shift demonstrates a rich point about the tradition behind the Gospels, and how that tradition was regarded: The stories that go to make up the Gospels were handed down in the early Christian communities as independent units, each one carefully transmitted for itself before they were joined together "like pearls on a string" to form a continuous Gospel. The stories would be repeated for a particular purpose, to make a particular point or settle a particular question that was relevant to the life of the community at the time. When the Gospels came to be written, each evangelist arranged the pearls on the string in his own order.

That the evangelists arranged the incidents in their own order does not cast doubt on the historicity of the incidents themselves. In fact, in the search for the bedrock of the Jesus tradition, this controversy is an example of one important principle, sometimes called by scholars the Friend-and-Foe Criterion: Something accepted by Jesus' foes as well as by his friends is especially strongly grounded in history. By attributing his miracles to Beelzebul, Jesus' opponents implicitly accepted that his miracles did in fact happen, and needed explanation.

Beelzebul was a name for a popular evil spirit (meaning "Lord of the Frontier," but often distorted by opponents into the mocking "Beelzebub" or "Lord of the Flies"). The fact that Jesus replies with a reflection on the kingdom suggests that the original context was not merely a gibe about his exorcisms, but a wider accusation against the kingdom that he was proclaiming. His opponents must have claimed that this was not the kingdom of God at all, but the kingdom of an evil spirit. This, too, is an important friend-or-foe consequence: Both sides accept that the central point of Jesus' activity is not isolated exorcisms but the wider implication of those exorcisms, that Jesus has come to announce the blossoming of the sovereignty of God in a new way.

Luke and the Three-piece Suite

THE LITTLE PARABLE about the evil spirits taking over a house has plenty to tell us about Luke and his circumstances. Mark's version is very simple: A robber enters a house to steal some tools and ties up the muscular owner. It is simply a pair with the previous parable, to reinforce that a household or kingdom can have only one master. Luke shows us an owner (representing any human being) standing guard, armed to the teeth to protect his possessions; now it is a question of what you value in life, where your heart is. The confrontation is such that the stronger man can be said to have "won a victory." Then he takes away the weaponry on which the householder was relying and scatters around all the cherished possessions. It is not a simple burglary of a few tools but the systematic devastation of a comfortable residence. And when the seven spirits, worse than himself, join the original tough guy, one can imagine them lounging with their dirty boots on the sofa, stubbing out their cigarettes on the carpet. If possessions are so important to Luke's audience, one can see why he needs to warn against being distracted by them from the more important concerns of God's kingdom.

The Blessed Mother

THIS PREOCCUPATION WITH possessions receives a stark contrast with the simplicity of the blessing on the womb and breasts of Jesus' mother, a touching emphasis on the normality of his humanity. Yet Jesus replies that the blessing on a mother is not to be compared with the blessing on those who respond to the word of God. This is not to be read as any disrespect for his mother on Jesus' part, but, rather, as an expression of the central task of the disciple: to hear the word of God.

REFLECTION
Who is master in my house? Ambition, possessions, sex, comfort, my good name, my next holiday—or the word of God?

JESUS' COUNTERATTACK

The Sign of Jonah

THE ATTACK OF the opponents had been double—the accusation of alliance with Beelzebul and the demand for a sign. Jesus has already answered the first, and now proceeds to the second: The only sign to be given is the sign of Jonah. There seem to have been different points of view about the sign. In Mark 8:12 (surely the earliest version) Jesus gives an entirely negative response, abruptly and with an oath refusing any sign from heaven. They were perhaps wanting a direct intervention from God, in the form of a pronouncement or voice from heaven, such as was given at the baptism. In Matthew 12:40 Jesus reverses this by promising a sign, the resurrection: "For as Jonah remained in the belly of the sea monster for three days and three nights, so will the Son of Man be in the heart of the earth for three days and three nights." Between these two positions falls Luke. There is no mention of the three days in the sea monster as an interpretation of the resurrection after three days, but, rather, the sign of Jonah is understood as his preaching of repentance. Jesus' own preaching of repentance is compared to that of Jonah. The difference lies in the response: The men of Nineveh responded to the preaching of Jonah, in contrast to the present generation. Similarly the queen of Sheba responded with her admiration to the wisdom of Solomon. Both (note Luke's usual pairing of male and female) will come forward at the judgment in witness against those who failed to respond to the one who was greater than the wisdom of Solomon and more forceful than the preaching of Jonah.

Parables of Light

THREE SHORT PARABLES on light follow. The general idea of the first must be that the preaching of Jesus is a lamp that can be clearly seen. The second is about clarity of vision in the beholder, and so is a reflection on the acceptance of the message. It makes use of the physiology that the eye is a receptor of light by which light penetrates the body, provided that the eye does not contain a blockage. The third saying combines the two, linking the idea of a lamp shining with that of the body penetrated and transformed by light.

Rebuke to the Pharisees and Lawyers

FINALLY LUKE BUILDS the conventional Hellenistic scene of a meal as an occasion of conversation and teaching to give a general tableau of criticism of the Pharisees and lawyers. He uses much of the material that comes in the indictment of the scribes and Pharisees in Matthew 23, but instead of lumping them together, Luke separates the charges appropriately. First come three charges against the Pharisees, that they fuss about ritual cleansing rather than generosity, that they are concerned with paying the tithe on minute herbs while neglecting the love of God, that they are avid for human recognition and important seats in the synagogue. These are personal faults in the way they live.

Then attention turns to the lawyers, those who teach how the law should be observed; against them there are also three charges. They are charged with teaching others to carry burdens they themselves would not touch, and with taking away the key of knowledge, that is, of preventing even the well-intentioned from embracing this knowledge. But the weightiest of all the charges against the teachers of Israel is the central one of persistently refusing to recognize the prophets. This is applied to the past, the present, and—with the addition of "apostles"—the future. With all solemnity "the Wisdom of God" pronounces that this generation will pay the penalty. Luke is thinking both of the failure to recognize the prophets of the Old Testament, and especially of the failure to recognize Jesus the prophet and his apostles.

The letter of James says, "only a few of you . . . should be teachers"; to be a teacher of religion (and we all teach by example and in countless other ways of which we are unaware at the time) is a dangerous occupation. It demands especial sensitivity to the wisdom of God.

PRAYER

Lord, help me to see not whether but how all these charges apply to me in various ways. Open my eyes and give me courage to change what should be changed.

COURAGE IN THE
FACE OF PERSECUTION

IN THE TEACHING of Jesus, which Luke so cleverly disposes in his travel narrative, he constantly has his eye on the Church of the future and its apostolate. Here he first puts forward a dramatic contrast between the authorities of the Jews who lie in wait to catch Jesus out (11:54), and the crowds who are so enthusiastic that some of their number get trampled (12:1). There is a steady contrast between the positive response of the populace and the negative response of their leaders. This is mirrored in the Passion narrative, where the leaders deliver Jesus up, while the people engage in an act of sorrow that almost amounts to a liturgy of repentance. In the Acts of the Apostles, too, the opposition of the leaders becomes ever stronger, while increasing thousands of the people join the new movement.

An Apostolate Under Persecution

AS A PROPHET, Luke's Jesus is clearly speaking about the task of the apostles after his death and resurrection. The first point he makes is that they are his friends: "To you my friends I say . . ." Nowhere else in Luke are they so addressed. The address immediately recalls John 15:14: At the Last Supper Jesus is speaking of the future of the Church, and of their need to remain united to him as branches to the vine, when he says, "You are my friends, if you do what I command you. I shall no longer call you servants, because a servant does not know the master's business; I call you friends, because I have made known to you everything I have learned from my Father." It is as the trusted friends of Jesus that his apostles are sent out.

The second important point is that Jesus sends them out in the full knowledge that they will be persecuted and killed. This foreknowledge is constantly stressed. They will be taken before synagogues and magistrates and (somewhat vaguer) authorities, as indeed in the Acts the apostles are taken before the synagogue rulers, as Paul is taken before magistrates in

Philippi and Corinth, and before the Roman authorities at Caesarea. The same sort of prediction is made by the prophet Agabus in Acts 21:11 as Paul prepares to go up to Jerusalem toward his imprisonment. Despite this, Jesus assures them of their value and the protection they will receive. Of all the qualities he recommends, perhaps Luke puts most emphasis on perseverance, the ability to hang on in the face of persecution.

A touching little parallel to this is the saying of the Galilean teacher Rabbi Simeon ben Yohai when threatened with capture by the Romans half a century later: "Not even a bird perishes without the will of heaven. How much less a Son of Man." Not only is there a parallel with the care of five sparrows worth only two bronze coins, but also a parallel in the mysterious expression (which seems to have been characteristic of Jesus' speech, for in the New Testament it comes only on his lips), "The Son of Man," as referring to himself.

Blasphemy Against the Spirit

THE SAYING ABOUT blasphemy against the Spirit is truly puzzling. In Mark 3:29 and Matthew 12:32 it comes as part of Jesus' reply to the accusation that he cast out evil spirits by Beelzebul. Why the distinction between the two kinds of blasphemy (possibly to be understood as "abuse")? Is Jesus less sacred than the Spirit? However, by putting the saying into this context Luke does perhaps suggest a particular sense: the failure of many to recognize Jesus during his earthly ministry may be forgiven, and even the failure of the disciples at the Passion. The preaching of the Acts of the Apostles is under the close guidance of the Spirit—it has been called the era of the Spirit—and by this preaching all are given a second chance, which many accept. It is the refusal to accept this preaching that can have no forgiveness.

PRAYER

Give me courage, Lord, to persevere in the face of hostility, mockery, and indifference. Give me the conviction that your message is worth persecution and death, that you never desert your messengers. Help me to remember how many sparrows I am worth.

THE DANGER OF POSSESSIONS

THIS WHOLE SECTION of the journey to Jerusalem is centered on discipleship. Luke has just given us the teaching of Jesus about facing persecution without fear. Now he warns against taking false refuge in the material security of possessions, a subject to which he often returns. Luke is the most insistent of the evangelists on God's special care for the poor, and on the danger of riches: These are a constant distraction from the true purpose of the disciple. The only way such danger can be removed is by using this apparent wealth to store up true wealth in heaven.

The teaching is introduced by a question from the crowd. The question about inheritance is stunningly insensitive after Jesus' previous teaching, but it forms a dramatic device often used by Luke, a question out of the blue, simply a starting point for the answer.

The Rich Fool

THE PARABLE OF the rich fool has been described as the most terrible of all the Gospel parables: Retribution is swift and absolute. The story is typical of Luke's parables. First, several of Luke's parables seem to be formed out of a short allusion in the Old Testament wisdom literature, and this parable has a close parallel in the book of Ecclesiasticus (11:18–20). Luke's story is a superb dramatization of this little vignette:

> *Others grow rich by pinching and scraping,*
>   *and here is the reward they receive for it:*
> *although they say, "Now I can sit back*
>   *and enjoy the benefit of what I have got,"*
> *they do not know how long this will last;*
>   *they will have to leave their goods to others and die.*

Many of Luke's parables have this sort of antihero instead of a hero, a disreputable character who nevertheless sometimes does the right thing for the wrong reason. Here Luke presents his antihero in a lifelike and witty manner, giving him a little monologue (another feature of Luke's antiheroes) about how he should get out of his comfortably tiresome situation of superfluity. The lip-smacking self-preoccupation is expressed in his referring to himself eight times in two verses! "What am *I* to do? *I* have not enough room to store *my* crops." Then he said, "This is what *I* will do: *I* will pull down *my* barns and build bigger ones, and store all *my* grain and *my* goods in them, and *I* will say to *my* soul: '*My* soul, *you* . . .'"

This is followed by a typically Lucan four-barrelled salvo, "take things easy, eat, drink, have a good time," just like the four different barrels to come in 14:21, "the poor, the crippled, the blind, and the lame," or in 21:16, "parents and brothers, relations and friends."

Trust in the Father

THE WORD "STOREHOUSE" links the parable to the teaching on trust that Matthew gives in the Sermon on the Mount: Ravens have no use for storehouses. In contrast to the rich man's preoccupation with his possessions, the natural world of ravens and flowers has no such worry but has equal splendor. Luke shares this lovely appreciation of nature with Matthew, but intensifies it in two ways. He stresses the fatherly care of God: The Father will give not only natural existence and growth but the kingdom as well.

He is also more radical and extreme than Matthew about dispossession. Matthew carefully covers his back with "Seek *first* the kingdom," which does not exclude attention to other things, though of course doing them second. Luke is more absolute. "Seek his kingdom and these things will be added to you," with no suggestion of a secondary search. Indeed, Luke encourages Christians positively to get rid of possessions. Possessions for Luke are a disadvantage and a danger: "Sell your possessions and give to those in need." It is attractive to see the "purses that do not wear out" as the beneficiaries of this giving, the poor who by their gratitude will function as treasure in heaven.

PRAYER
Lord, keep me alert to the danger of possessions, of attachment to unimportant things which distract me from the true search. Help me to share the pain of those in need and to help them in whatever way I can.

WAITING FOR THE RETURN

THE THIRD MAJOR section of this collection of instructions for disciples—after a major section on perseverance under trial and another on the danger of possessions—concerns continual alertness.

Paul makes clear, particularly in his early letters, 1 Thessalonians and 1 Corinthians, that the first generation of Christians vividly expected the risen Christ to come again like a victor in a triumphal procession, to gather Christians and take them with him to present the kingdom to his Father. Paul taught that Christ had overcome death, and that, for those who by baptism had united themselves to Christ's death and resurrection, death was no more. His argument in 1 Thessalonians 4:13–18 implies that some of the Thessalonians had understood this to mean that anyone who did die had lost the chance of joining Christ in his resurrection—an interpretation Paul is eager to correct. Paul's later letters, and especially Colossians and Ephesians, show much less interest in the return of Christ, and more interest in the transformation of the Christian that has already taken place through the Spirit. Similarly the fourth Gospel focuses on the enduring presence of Christ's Spirit among his disciples rather than on a future coming. The immediacy of the expectation waned as the second coming did not occur.

It is generally accepted that Luke is the latest of the Synoptic Gospels, written when it was becoming clear that the second coming was not to be so immediate as had originally been envisaged. So it is often said that he was at pains to deflect attention from the second coming in order to concentrate on the presence of the Spirit, now guiding the Church in all its activity and decisions, as is so fully apparent in the narrative of Acts. There is little sign of this tendency in this section of the Gospel; it falls into two parts.

The Watchful Servants

THE FIRST SECTION is directed toward all disciples, and is centered around two little images, the first illustrating endurance and the second unexpectedness. The first of the two makes an interesting combination: The servants must be ready for energetic action when the master of the house comes home from a wedding. It is perhaps slightly surprising that the master then sits the servants down and proceeds to serve them a meal, even though he comes well after midnight! Nevertheless, it is a warm testimony of his affection for them and his response to their wakefulness. In the second image the master of the household is himself on the watch, and this time for burglars, digging through the mud-brick wall of his house—or, rather, if he had been on the watch, he would have prevented the burglar.

The Trustworthy Steward

THE SECOND SECTION turns attention to those with authority in the community, as Peter's interjection suggests. It presents two opposing pictures, the one of the steward of the household who sees his office as service and is duly rewarded with promotion, the other of the steward who takes the opportunity of his master's delay to domineer and terrorize the junior members of the household and to make free with his master's goods. The gentle act of service offered by the former is surely reminiscent of Jesus himself at the Last Supper. The behavior of the latter resembles that of the rich fool, though rather worse; at any rate, the rich fool stopped short of drunkenness!

Finally comes a careful little codicil, unique to Luke, giving a graded scale of punishment. The more you know, the worse your punishment; the greater the gift, the greater the penalty. Whom does Luke envisage? Is it a warning to the leaders of the Christian community, or a threat to the leaders of the Jews? The final saying has a distinctly Semitic ring, which could stem from Jesus, literally, "To everyone to whom much has been given, much will be asked [theological passive, avoiding use of God's name] from him [again a Semitic construction]; to whom much has been entrusted, they will ask [impersonal plural] more from him."

PRAYER

Lord, keep me alert to your coming, and aware that I must render to you an account of my stewardship. Give me a true conception of service to those whom I reach. Keep me from the easy tyranny of bullying those whom I should serve.

A CALL FOR DECISION

Fire on the Earth

AT THE END of this long series of teachings on the conditions and consequences of being a disciple comes the challenge for decision. The challenge is presented in a series of images, only two of which (division in households and the law court scene) come also in Matthew.

When Jesus says that he has come to throw fire on the earth, it could mean that he is reverting to the message of John the Baptist. His message was one of purifying fire that would burn away the impurities. Or is the saying to be related to the fire of the Holy Spirit? At Pentecost the Spirit is represented by tongues of fire, and the baptism with the Spirit is a baptism with fire. In the Bible, fire is often the symbol of the presence of God, as at the burning bush or the pillar of fire in the desert. Inevitably this is a fire that purifies as well as fills with enthusiasm and ardor.

Baptism also has a natural symbolism, clarified by the saying of Jesus to the sons of Zebedee in Mark 10:38, "Can you drink the cup that I must drink and be baptized with the baptism with which I must be baptized?" Literally baptism means "being dipped" in water. To the Hebrew mind, water was the abode of evil spirits and evil, uncontrollable passions. To be dipped in it was a kind of death and dissolution, inevitably painful; to rise from it was to rise to a new and purified life. However Jesus understood his death under this image, the saying must show that he is eager to complete his task. To the evangelist this means the advance to the life of Christ in the Christian community.

Division

IT IS ONLY too clear that not all will accept the call to follow Christ. Elsewhere (Luke 14:26) Jesus says that loyalty to him must exceed even those natural family loyalties that are most dear and cherished. Here he is perhaps more extreme in promising actual strife in the household, a strife that the cumbersome English expressions make to sound even more chaotic! And this is not just during a short family visit for Christmas. In the Palestinian household, no doubt all these family members lived permanently together, so that the strife between those who chose to follow Christ and those who did not was a permanent condition of existence. The price of discipleship must be faced squarely.

Warning Signs

THE TWO CONCLUDING images of weather and law court are quite puzzling because they are never explained. By their position, however, it is clear that they must be challenges to decision while there is still time. The signs of change in weather are quite reliable in Palestine and any skilled and careful country-man can read them. But why the charge of hypocrisy? It suggests that the opponents of Jesus were perfectly aware of the meaning of the signs and simply chose to ignore them.

The law court challenge is not a challenge to take the law into one's own hands. Rather, it must be seen as a challenge to accept what is inevitable, instead of blinding oneself by hoping against hope that it will never happen. The long-drawn-out process of being passed from one official to another merely introduces to the scene the impression of a slow-motion inevitability, not any hope that it will not happen in the end. Matthew applies a slightly shortened version of this law court scene in the literal sense of the need to be reconciled with neighbors. Luke, however, may have retained the original sense of the need for decision in time of crisis. Perhaps the original challenge was to recognize the coming of Jesus as the time of decision, which is applied by the evangelist to each disciple's personal decision.

PRAYER

Lord, you have warned me. To follow you is demanding.
You demand that my whole life should be focused on you. You take away
from me all the evasions of comfort and luxury. You demand that I serve
all those around me, as you served your disciples. You warn me of strife
and division. You want a decision now and every day. You offer me the
fire of your Spirit and the life of your baptism, and you promise finally
to claim me for your own before your Father.

TIME FOR REPENTANCE

THE SPECIFIC SECTION on the demands and tensions of discipleship is finished, and Luke now turns attention to a subject that applies more generally, the need to recognize guilt and to repent of it. First come two historical examples of sudden death without chance to repent. These may have been well-known and standard examples at the time, but they have left no other trace in history. Then comes the example of the fig tree, representing a breathing space left for repentance. Both situations show the need for a radical change of direction in the lives of most of us in order to embrace Christ wholeheartedly. The Hebrew word for "repent" means simply "to turn back," the Greek "to change one's mind or attitude or mind-set." The follower of Christ sees all things differently and strives to act accordingly.

Pilate

THE MENTION OF Pilate here, besides giving a useful historical example, is surely an allusive preparation for his appearance later in the Passion narrative. The incident here mentioned is otherwise unknown, but the way it is described, mingling their blood with that of their sacrifices, suggests an unfeeling brutality, even sadism. This is certainly the picture of Pilate provided by Jewish historians, but then, it is in the interests of Josephus and Philo to represent the Roman governors of Judea as tyrannical beasts who goaded even the placid, well-intentioned Jews to revolt. Pilate disappears from the stage of history when his superior, the governor of Syria, sends him to Rome to explain his excessive severity in putting down a messianic revolt in Samaria in A.D. 36. Any number of reconstructions of this case is possible, and any number of studies of Pilate's psychology and history has been made. From the evidence offered by Josephus it can certainly be argued that the politically adept leaders of the Jews repeatedly made a fool of him by the skilled manipulation of their incomprehensible religious taboos. For Luke's example of sudden death, Pilate's motivation and behavior are, in any case, unimportant.

Nor is anything more known about the collapse of the tower at Siloam. The pool of Siloam still exists in the ancient city of David, the oldest part of Jerusalem. Water is carried to it from the only spring of Jerusalem, by an amazing underground tunnel in the rock, over 1,800 feet long, chiseled out 2,600 years ago. The slopes of the hill around Siloam are steep enough for the collapse of a tower not to be surprising, and the habitations are so densely packed that such a collapse could well have wreaked considerable damage.

The Barren Fig Tree

THE STORY OF the barren fig tree again takes us forward to the Passion. In Mark the episode of the cleansing of the temple is sandwiched between Jesus' curse on a fig tree that has no fruit and the observation by the disciples that it has already withered. The fig tree is therefore the symbol of the barrenness of Israel, serving to point the moral of Jesus' action in the temple. In Luke the incident provides material for this parable. The meaning of the fig tree is reinforced by its being placed (somewhat incongruously) in a vineyard, for the vineyard also is a symbol of Israel; we have, therefore, a double symbol of Israel. The lesson of the story is, however, in this case less specifically attached to Israel than generalized to show that the Lord offers time for repentance.

Three Years

THIS IS THE only mention of three years in the Gospel, and it is fascinating to speculate whether it was this that gave rise to the widespread tradition that Jesus' ministry lasted three years. The only other evidence that enters into discussion is the three mentions of the Passover in the fourth Gospel. In fact, this evidence is quite unclear: These need not have been separate Passovers, and there may have been others during Jesus' ministry that are not recorded. The fact is that we do not know how long his ministry lasted; it could have been more than three years or less.

PRAYER

Lord, you have given me time to repent and to change my priorities to accord with yours. Help me to see how I should change my mind-set, how I need to turn back to your welcoming embrace.

HEALINGS ON A SABBATH

THESE TWO HEALINGS form a pair. This is not unexpected in Luke, who so often pairs men and women. They are the more striking in that they are the only healing miracles to occur in this part of the Gospel. The clue is given because each is introduced by the same phrase: "there before him was a woman . . ."; "there in front of him was a man . . ." Each occurs on a sabbath, each includes a dialogue with the Jewish authorities about whether it is legitimate to heal on a sabbath in which Jesus uses the classic rabbinic argument a fortiori: If it is legitimate to help a beast of burden on a sabbath, it is allowable to help a human being. Each ends with the discomfiture of Jesus' opponents. Matthew has a similar story in 12:9–14, but in his equivalent to that story Luke (6:6–11) follows Mark and gives no carefully wrought legal argument.

The question that arises from these stories is what Jesus was aiming to do. The careful form of argumentation remains within the acceptable bounds of legal debate. Jesus is merely putting forward one interpretation, which might or might not be accepted, but would certainly not count as rejection of the whole legal system. How radical was Jesus? Matthew 24:20 ("Pray that you will not have to make your escape . . . on a sabbath") suggests that the sabbath was still kept in his community, and the dispute over observance of the food laws in the early Church (especially the fierce altercation at Antioch between Peter and Paul) suggests that at first they were retained. On the other hand, other actions of Jesus, such as his purging of the temple and his removal of the limited permission to divorce, do suggest that his renewal of the Law was radical. Again other sayings, "the Son of Man is master even of the sabbath," suggest that his mastery and renewal of the Law were personal, and that he was chiefly asserting his personal authority. It is difficult to make a definite decision between these points of view. Each is supported by reputable contemporary scholars.

For Luke the emphasis of the story of the woman is on Jesus' pity for her, contrasting with the niggardliness of the president of the synagogue. This must be the meaning of the double emphasis on her symptoms ("bent double and quite unable to stand upright"), the gentle description of her as a "daughter of Abraham," and again the double mention of being set free (vv. 12, 16). It is also a means of glorifying God, as both the woman and the crowd do. The story of the man is much shorter and more skeletal, so that the only real impression one gets is of the sullen stubbornness of Jesus' opponents, watching him silently and refusing to offer any answer either to Jesus' arguments or to the miracle itself.

Parables of the Mustard Seed and the Leaven

THESE TWO SHORT parables, again pairing male and female ("mustard seed which a man took . . ."; "yeast a woman took . . ."), are placed by Luke in a different context to Mark and Matthew. Mark does not have the parable of the leaven; it is added to the mustard seed by Matthew, who likes to emphasize the point by giving parables in pairs. Their original meaning in Jesus' mouth fits one of two possibilities. Either they could be in answer to opponents who mock a claim that such an unimpressive group could be the overwhelming kingdom of God. Or the context could be disappointment and depression on the part of the disciples at their seeming lack of success. To each situation Jesus replies with the image of paradoxical growth: Just wait and see!

These two parables of promise and progress conclude the first part of the travel narrative with a hopeful and positive image. They make the point that the kingdom is even then spreading as Jesus passes on his journey. There follows immediately the second mention of Jerusalem (v. 22), the first geographical indication we have had since 9:51.

PRAYER
Lord, as we travel through life on the way to our Jerusalem,
many things happen to us in seemingly haphazard sequence. I cannot
follow all that you are planning for me. Grant that I may stop every now
and then to reflect that the mustard seed you have planted and the
leaven you have hidden are both growing silently toward the completion
you design for them.

53 LUKE 13:22-35

JESUS SETS HIS FACE TO JERUSALEM

BY CONTRAST TO the geographical "weightlessness" that is characteristic of the great journey to Jerusalem, here we set foot on solid ground with the mention of Jerusalem three separate times. It is a thorough reminder, at the midpoint stage, of the purpose of the journey. The whole section is full of foreboding, becoming more and more tragic as it progresses. This group of first warnings against Israel prepares for the great laments over Jerusalem and its failure to respond, which Jesus pronounces as he arrives in and finally leaves Jerusalem.

Warnings to Israel

LUKE HERE GROUPS several warnings that come separately in Matthew. The section comprising verses 22–30 is bound together by the idea of the difficulty of salvation. First comes the warning about the narrow door. Then, for Luke, the idea of the narrow door leads on to that of the closed door. The scene is made more touching by the pleas of those who are shut out: "We once ate and drank in your company; you taught in our streets" (note Luke's interest in parties, and his stress on Jesus' role as a teacher). Of course, in trying to persuade the Lord of their close relationship to him, they succeed only in making matters worse. If they have shared table fellowship with him and listened to his teaching, it makes their failure to respond even more blatant. In a later age Christians might reflect on the listening to the word of God and the table fellowship that occur in the eucharist. The Lord's reply is all the sterner: He repeats (v. 27) the phrase in verse 25, "I do not know you."

Finally comes a warning Luke has reserved from the story of the centurion's boy (Luke 7), where he omitted a couple of verses given in Matthew 8:11–12. But there is an important difference. One theme of Matthew's Gospel is that the kingdom will be taken away from the Jews and given to a new people of God, so there Jesus says, "The children of the kingdom will be thrown out into the darkness outside." Luke does not want to condemn the Jews to such wholesale failure. He always makes a sharp distinction between the leaders and the people as a whole; the former fail to respond, but the latter are sympathetic to Jesus. So it is only "all evildoers" who are excluded. The main point is the more expansive one of admitting those who come from east and west, from north and south. The time has come for the admission of the Gentiles, and it is more important to include than to exclude.

Herod the Fox

"THAT FOX," SAYS Jesus. According to the Jewish historian Josephus, Herod the Tetrarch, ruler of Galilee, worked as an informer for the Romans, keeping the authorities abreast of what was going on. This would not have increased his popularity among his own people. However, the main point of this little passage is twofold: We are informed once more that Jesus knows clearly the fate that lies in store for him, and it is as a prophet that he goes up to Jerusalem to perish there. On every level Jesus' move to Jerusalem was no chance journey. He had to fulfill his prophetic mission to Judaism at its center, at the temple. Otherwise it would be incomplete. It was only at Jerusalem that he could make the definitive prophetic gesture to lay bare the barrenness of the temple and its cult.

Lament for Jerusalem

JESUS' LOVE FOR and care of Jerusalem elicit two laments, one now, at the halfway point of the journey, and one immediately after the entry to Jerusalem (to which he now alludes, for it is then that they will say, "Blessed is he who is coming in the name of the Lord!"). But such yearning for Jerusalem lies deep in every Jewish heart.

It is valuable to point out that the feminine and motherly affection of the hen is not out of place in the mouth of the man Jesus. God's own love can be expressed in the same terms: "As a mother comforts a child, so shall I comfort you" (Isaiah 66:13).

PRAYER
How often have I longed to gather your children together as a hen gathers her brood under her wings!

GUESTS FOR DINNER

NOW, AFTER ANOTHER story of healing on a sabbath (discussed a little earlier in section 52), Luke gives three parables about invitations to dinner. This framework would be, perhaps, too formal for Mark's rustic world, but in Luke's more cultured Hellenistic world a dinner is often used as an occasion for teaching. Luke has used it importantly already in the house of Simon the Pharisee (7:36–50), and will so use it again at the Last Supper, where he places important teaching of Jesus about the leadership of the future community and the perseverance that will be needed. The present parables are about invitations rather than about the scene of a supper itself. The heavily critical tone, however, fits the present scene: The host is "one of the leading Pharisees" (v. 1), and Jesus is speaking to "lawyers and Pharisees" (v. 3).

Places at Table

THE FIRST PARABLE is on humility, or knowing one's place, a condition of discipleship. This is an important quality; the parable of the Pharisee and the tax collector will suggest that it is important especially as a precondition of repentance.

This is another occasion when we see the genius so often demonstrated in Luke's parables of picking up a hint and turning it into a brilliant little story. Matthew (23:6) contents himself with the bare comment that the scribes and Pharisees want to take the places of honor at banquets. As the parable of the rich fool is related to a saying in the wisdom literature, this parable, too, may well be linked to Proverbs 25:6–7: "Do not take a place among the great; better to be invited, 'Come up here,' than be humiliated in the presence of the prince." As so often in the Old Testament wisdom literature itself, there is a certain worldly wisdom about the story. Luke's characters are certainly not above doing the right thing for the wrong reason! Christians will benefit from the lesson in knowing one's place, but it is a lesson that applies beyond the circle of Christian discipleship.

There is even a neat and slightly crafty lesson on how to get on in the world, as we often see in wisdom literature! It is only the final stark sentence—with its two "theological passives" to avoid using the name of God—that hammers home the specifically Christian message about which conduct will finally win its reward, and shows that the story really is a parable rather than a straight piece of advice about how most safely to get the best places: "Everyone who raises himself up will be humbled, and the one who humbles himself will be raised up."

It is also characteristic of Luke to make much of this motif of shame and honor. So the crafty steward is prevented by shame from relying on begging; the friend at midnight gets what he wants by shouting out shamelessly and so shaming his friend. The incautious tower builder is made fun of (14:29). Here the parable builds on the model in Proverbs, painting both humiliation and honor with characteristic liveliness.

The Neglected Are Privileged

BESIDES THE LESSON to the guests, there is also a lesson for the host, and this time not one about spiritual dispositions but a practical message of inviting those who cannot repay. As so often the gospel message is socially firmly subversive, the more so because the lame, the blind, and the crippled are excluded from the community meal in the regulations of the Scrolls of Qumran (1 QSa 2). The poor, the crippled, the lame, the blind, form another Lucan set of four, who will occur also in the next parable (v. 21).

The cozy closed circle of reciprocal invitations is deeply ingrained also in our modern social conventions, but Jesus' instructions here are not merely not to perpetuate it but deliberately to shatter it: Do not make a habit of inviting your friends etc., *in case they* return the invitation. The circle must be kept open by a deliberate act of avoidance of the return invitation. There is a nice touch of wit in the final sentence: The return invitation comes only to the heavenly banquet!

PRAYER
*Lord, keep me clear of any covert self-seeking in what I
pretend to be generosity. Let me truly give without hope of reward. Give
me real affection and tenderness for those who lack the good things of
the world, remembering that they are your privileged friends.*

THE GREAT SUPPER

THE THIRD PARABLE about a dinner is that of the great supper. One interest of this story is that the basic form is shared with Matthew, though the details and the use are very different. It is from a comparison of the details that Luke's purpose may be discerned, for both Matthew and Luke show their emphasis by making some details (different in each case) allegorical.

We start with Matthew. For Matthew the story is of a marriage feast for the son of the king. This is an obvious allegory, for the prophets had long looked forward to the wedding feast at the end of time when the marriage between God and Israel would finally be celebrated with carefree merriment and plenty of all kinds. Now the wedding feast has become that of God's Son, a clear allegory for Jesus. The invited wedding guests are the Jews, who at the last moment refuse the invitation that had long been destined to them. They insult and kill the messengers—quite unnecessarily, except that the messengers stand for the prophets of Israel, who were traditionally maltreated. The king's overreaction in sending armies to burn their city (odd that they all lived in the same city!) makes better sense in the application to Jerusalem than it would in a more realistic story. The overall meaning suits exactly Matthew's message, that the kingdom is to be taken away from Israel and given to another nation.

Luke's story is slightly but significantly different. There is only one messenger, who, not being a prophet, does not need to be maltreated and killed. The invited guests do not simply slope off wordlessly to their field and their shop. Instead, they have a little dialogue, full of urbane Oriental courtesy. The explicitness of their excuses enables us to see more clearly that it is the distractions of possession that block their acceptance of the invitation. Luke also adds a third blockage, marriage, which is several times represented as danger in Luke.

The really significant change, however, is in the replacements. In Matthew anyone will do to fill up the place. Luke is more specific; for him there are two groups. First come Luke's favored quartet, the poor, the crippled, the lame, the blind. So the first guests at the banquet of the kingdom are to be the underpriviledged on earth: "Blessed are you who are hungry now: You shall have your fill." Equally significant is the second group, for which the slave has to go outside the city into the open roads and hedgerows. The city must, of course, represent the Chosen People, and the sending of the messenger outside the city represents an extension of the pressing invitation to include the Gentiles. Unlike Matthew, who sees the Jews as having been totally replaced by a new nation, Luke insists that some of the Jews respond to the call, and that it is extended from them to the Gentiles.

Counting the Cost

AFTER THE PARABLE, Luke makes clear just how demanding is the call. This is perhaps the toughest formulation in all the Gospels. Matthew's version is gentler in two respects: He has "whoever *loves* father or mother, son or daughter more than me . . ." (RSV), whereas Luke goes further: "Anyone who comes to me *without hating* . . ."; and Matthew does not include "wife" among the relations, whereas Luke does. We cannot accept that Christian discipleship actually demands hate within the family. To "hate" a wife is the most paradoxical of all demands.

A step toward understanding this awesome demand may be that Semitic thought-forms and language are weak in the comparatives "more" and "less" and tend to express preferences in absolute terms. The lesson must be that even the warmest and closest of all human ties of affection must give way before loyalty to Christ. Rather than a way of weakening human family ties, it takes the most vibrant of bonds to show that the bond to Christ must be even stronger.

The warning is reinforced by the two parables of calculation before setting out on a task. They are paralleled in no other Gospel text and could well be parables of popular wisdom. At the end of them Luke again repeats his demand of total abandonment of possessions (v. 33). It is only in Luke's Gospel that we are carefully told at the call of each disciple that they give up "everything."

PRAYER
Lord, you don't help me to count the cost, for how can I
know what the cost will be? You just demand simply that I put you
before everything, that nothing at all may count besides you. No
bargaining. No calculating. Give me the strength and courage to render
you this fiercest of loyalties.

LOST SHEEP AND LOST COIN

NOW LUKE HAS three parables of repentance, the first two of which form a pair. Again the comparison with Matthew is illuminating. To begin with, Matthew has only one to Luke's two. Luke's are very similar to each other, even in language. It may be that the doubling up has two purposes, first to emphasize by repetition, and second to pair man and woman: A man loses the sheep, a woman the coin.

The Lost Sheep

MATTHEW'S PARABLE OF the lost sheep comes in his chapter 18 on the community and the duties of its members to one another. So the emphasis is on the duty of every member of the community to go to look for a lost sheep. In Luke the emphasis is on the shepherd's enduring search: He goes on looking till he has found the missing sheep. The shepherd, of course, is God, who is repeatedly represented in the Old Testament as the shepherd of his people. The very search itself is an expression of desperation: It can hardly be considered good husbandry to leave ninety-nine sheep free to wander off over the hills and fall down the precipices so frequent in Palestine. In desperation logic comes second! (In John's parable of the good shepherd there is a similar fault of logic: A good shepherd has no business getting himself killed, even if he is sacrificing himself for the sheep.) The affection of the shepherd is already seen in the contrast with Matthew: In Matthew the sheep wanders off, whereas in Luke the shepherd loses his sheep. Once the sheep has been found, the overwhelming reaction is delight as the shepherd shows his affection for the sheep and calls his friends and neighbors together—with a typical little bit of Lucan direct speech.

The Lost Coin

THE STORY OF the lost coin runs on the same lines. A small Palestinian sugar-lump house would be ill lit, perhaps with no entrance for light except the doorway. Lighting a lamp was not enough! The best way to find anything on the uneven, mud-lined floor would be to sweep it. Again the woman's joy is out of all reasonable proportion. A drachma was the Greek equivalent of a Roman denarius, so a day's wage of a casual agricultural laborer. The party for all these friends and neighbors would be bound to cost more than the drachma she had found. But the point of the two stories is precisely to show that the joy in heaven (again, a way of avoiding using the name of God) cannot be calculated according to any scale of reason.

Repentance

THE TWO PARABLES illustrate well the precise point that must have annoyed the Pharisees and scribes who murmur at Jesus welcoming sinners and eating with them: Nothing seems to be said about repentance as a precondition. They seem to be still sinners when he eats with them, just as, in the stories, there is no possibility of interrogating the sheep or the coin about repentance before it is brought back to the party in triumph. Is it pressing the imagery too far to maintain that the sheep and the coin remain merely passive and unchanged? It cannot be that the sinners continue forever as sinners, and repentance and conversion have a crucial part to play. This is another vital difference between the stories in Matthew and in Luke: In Matthew the emphasis is so strictly on the duty of brothers to look after one another that there is no mention of change of heart, and the conclusion is "It is never the will of your Father in heaven that one of these little ones should be lost." In Luke the repentance is stressed in each story. But it is important that Jesus is prepared to eat with them while they are still sinners. He does not wait for their conversion before going to join them; the conversion comes only when he is with them. He does not avoid the company of sinners, and his presence must transform them. This is an illustration not of his tolerance of sin, but of his love for sinners. The joy of the two finders contrasts forcefully with the niggardly grumpiness of the Pharisees and scribes.

PRAYER
Lord Jesus, help me to respond to your openness and welcome. You do not demand immediate perfection, but by your affection draw me gently back to your fold. Enable me, too, to show the same encouragement to others.

THE PRODIGAL SON

THIS THIRD PARABLE of repentance and forgiveness has had difficulty finding a title. Should it be "the prodigal son," "the forgiving father," or even "the powerless father" (because he is so helplessly affectionate)? Luke's story is told with all the delicacy and character of his artistry. The story is told with a fine balance, the geographical movements away and back neatly parallel to each other, and symbolizing the breaking and mending of the relationship. The son is lost—the son is found. The son loses everything—the son receives everything. In the center of all is the son's repentance.

The Younger Son

THE AUDACITY OF the younger son is breathtaking. He treats his father as virtually dead already. Not only the insult, but the financial loss: Presumably the father has to sell up half his property to provide the wastrel with his cash. The lowest point to which he sinks is, of course, tending unclean animals and even envying them. Luke is a realist and knows the usefulness of some such jolt toward repentance. This is a classic case of the Lucan antihero doing the right thing for the wrong reason. It is then that he is forced to take stock, and breaks out into that feature of so many of Luke's parables, a little puzzled speech to himself about what he should do (just like the rich fool, the crafty steward, or the unjust judge).

The Elder Son

THE PORTRAIT OF the elder son is also masterly. His resentment after all his years of loyal labor is utterly justified on any ordinary human level. No doubt he had had to work all the harder both for lack of his brother's labor and to make up for the sale of half the property. And, after all, the calf *we* had been fattening (yes, I've been working at that too) was part of his own share of the property. So he refuses even to acknowledge his brother; he calls him "this son of yours." Quite without justification he introduces "loose women" into the equation, though there has been no indication that they were among the wastrel's excesses. This detail is due entirely to the elder brother's own malice and jealousy. But then his anger is so well justified that the slight exaggeration of a carelessly chosen word is not surprising.

The Father

WELL, PERHAPS HE was a bit too indulgent at the beginning. He accepts the insult and the impoverishment—but then, most parents and superiors have to learn when to bite their tongues. It is not always helpful to tell home truths to the young. (St Paul agreed: ". . . everything is permissible, but not everything builds people up." [1 Corinthians 10:23]) When the first dust of the son's arrival appears on the horizon, the father *runs* to meet him, affection overcoming the demands of dignity in an Oriental gentleman who is no longer young. He embraces the son and will not even listen to the nice little prepared speech, which is interrupted in the middle, no doubt smothered in the embrace. He reassures the wastrel that all is forgiven and that trust is restored by even giving him the authority of a ring, so that he can sign away the rest of the property if he likes.

Nor is the resentful elder brother neglected: The celebration has begun when the father leaves his place at the head of the table, deserting his guests and newfound son, to go out and try to coax away his resentment. He has the generosity to acknowledge (and it takes courage to give ground to an angry man) that "all I have is yours." To the hurtful gibe "this son of yours," he replies gently with "your brother." A less generous story would have finished with a sharp contrast in the father's attitude to the two brothers and would have left the self-righteous elder brother to swelter in his own resentment. But this Father's affection is so limitless that even such behavior must be drawn back into love.

PRAYER

Father, I have the faults of both the brothers. Coax me always back into your love.

THE CRAFTY STEWARD

THE PREVIOUS PARABLES have been addressed to a combination of tax collectors and sinners, with Pharisees and scribes looking over their shoulders (15:1). Now Jesus turns to the other audience he has in the travel narrative, namely, the disciples.

The parable of the crafty steward has often been a shocking puzzle. Surely the master stands for God; how, then, can he praise the steward's astuteness? Here it is important to distinguish between parable and allegory. In an allegory each story detail has significance for the meaning. In a parable this is not the case, but there is only one point of direct comparison. Anyway, *is* the steward really dishonest in this case?

One explanation of the parable is that the steward simply remits to the debtors his own "cut," thereby earning their gratitude and friendship, which would be worth more to him than the short-term financial gain. It is a neat little move, and the master has the decency to approve; after all, he has himself lost nothing on the deal.

An alternative explanation is more complicated and specialized, relying on a knowledge of regional conditions. According to this, a clue to the wit of the parable is given by the different reductions of debt arranged by the steward. The debt of oil is halved, whereas the wheat is reduced only by one-fifth. The significance of this is that in some regions these are the standard interest rates charged. Oil is obviously easily adulterated with cheaper and undetectable liquids, so that a lender presumes that it will be adulterated and charges accordingly. Wheat is less easy to adulterate unobserved, so has a lower rate of return. In this case, the steward is merely remitting the interest to the debtors. But as lending at interest is against the Law of Moses, he is cleverly forcing his master to observe the Law, and the master can hardly complain. He should have acted more quickly and dismissed the steward in one swoop rather than giving him time to make his arrangements.

In either case, the steward behaves as a typical Lucan antihero, doing the right thing for the wrong reasons, and incidentally indulging in the little musing speech to himself as he wonders what he should do. The purpose of the parable is then to illustrate that the keenness with which we pursue our material objectives is often far more zealous than that devoted to "spiritual" ones.

Sayings on Money and Possessions

APPENDED TO THE parable are various sayings about money and possessions, not having any close connection with the parable itself, but, rather, tacked on at the end, linked only by the general subject matter. Luke has earlier given us one illustration of how money can be used to win friends, by the generosity of inviting those who cannot repay or reciprocate invitations (14:14). The conduct of the rich man toward Lazarus will soon give a counterillustration of failure to use money to win friends in the right way.

The three sayings on trustworthiness seem to be, rather, wisdom sayings about business life than part of the proclamation of the kingdom of God. The link to the parable is through the untrustworthiness of the steward. Further illustration of the reward of trustworthiness will be given later in the parable of the pounds. However, each of these sayings has the characteristic Lucan mistrust of money, "that tainted thing," that runs throughout the Gospel. It is the "little thing" contrasted with "great," and also presumably considered alien in the contrast of "what is not yours" with the power that transforms the self, "what is your very own."

Finally the saying on "mammon" has given rise to speculation that "Mammon" was the name of a deity, a god of money. There is nothing to support this, apart from the mention of two masters, which could suggest that Money and God can be put in rivalry to each other. But the whole meaning and derivation of the word are obscure. The word does not occur in the Old Testament, but appears sometimes in the Qumran literature in the normal sense of "money" or "wealth."

PRAYER
Lord, the variety of the sayings and warnings about money in the Gospel passage provides a mirror for the variety of ways in which money can prove a distraction or an insidious trap. Grant me to see the dangers of being seduced by the attractions of money, and to keep myself free to serve you.

THE RICH MAN AND LAZARUS

Various Sayings

IT IS NOT easy to see a pattern in the sayings of 16:14–18. The charge of avarice against the Pharisees links well to the previous section. It has been suggested that the link to the other sayings is provided by the words "loathsome (an abomination) in the sight of God" (v. 15); this could be a response to the jeering of the Pharisees at Jesus. The expression is used in the Old Testament for financial exploitation and for divorce, so it may provide a link between the two sayings in verses 15 and 18.

This would leave the two central of the four sayings (vv. 16, 17). The first of these announces that the kingdom is no longer confined to those envisaged in the Law and the prophets, for since John the Baptist "*everyone* is forcing their way into it." After this the saying on the continuance of the Law provides a counterbalance to retain the sanctity of the Law. The continuing relevance of it will be illustrated in the following story, in which Abraham refers to it explicitly.

The Rich Man and Lazarus

THE PARABLE IS told with a sparkling use of language typical of Luke's stylish writing. The rich man's invariable clothing ("he used to dress in . . .") is especially rich festal garb and his daily meal a glittering banquet, described in the words used for a very rare and special feast. By contrast, the poor man has been "thrown down" at the gate; the word used suggests that he has been dumped and cannot move. As dogs are unclean, the dogs licking his sores are intended to increase the disgust rather than (as a nation of dog lovers immediately assumes) to substitute for the human sympathy denied by the rich man.

The story is the perfect illustration of the reversal proclaimed in Luke's beatitudes and woes: "Alas for you who are rich: You are having your consolation now." This is made explicit in verse 25, when Lazarus has the consolation promised in the beatitudes. The exact meaning of the story is made clearer by comparison to a very similar ancient rabbinic story. In the rabbinic story the rich man is a tax collector, so inherently bad, and the poor man a student of the Law, so inherently good. Luke does not need these moral characteristics after his repeated lessons on the danger of wealth and the need to use it rightly; wealth and lack of it are enough to give the story its point. When both men get to the far side—note: The poor man's name means "God is my help"—the rich man is splendidly unrepentant. He still claims to be part of the Chosen People by calling out blithely, "Father Abraham," forgetting that John the Baptist has told us that it is not enough to claim Abraham as father (3:8). He still treats Lazarus as a servant who can be summarily sent as a messenger to render small services, and he actually has the effrontery to use the word for "pity" which forms part of the word for the "almsgiving" (eleeo and eleemosyne), which he had so signally failed to do.

When Abraham says the rich man's brothers can listen to the warnings of Moses and the prophets, he is referring to their constant teachings. One of the principal emphases of the moral teaching of the Law was the preservation of human dignity: Every human being must be dependent on God alone, without the humiliation, financial or legal, of being subject to another human. The prophets also, from Amos and Hosea onward, ceaselessly speak out against the exploitation of the poor by the rich. One entirely sympathizes with the sentiment that one more repetition of the warning would be useless. The irony of the rich man's final request is delicate: The Christian reader will immediately think of the resurrection proclamation of the apostles in the Acts (and the failure of the rich man's brothers to respond), whereas it is still possible that the rich man himself is thinking in pre-resurrection terms of a messenger from the dead, such as Samuel, who brought a warning message to Saul in 1 Samuel 28.

PRAYER

Lord, I am not destitute. I run the risk of your condemnation for failure to use properly the resources you have given me. Grant me discernment in my use of them. Above all, let me listen to your warnings and keep in mind the responsibility I bear.

A CHALLENGE TO DISCIPLES

THROUGHOUT THE NARRATIVE of the great journey, there has been an alternation between instructions to the crowds or Jesus' opponents and instructions to the disciples. Now, as we approach the end of the journey, comes a series of instructions to the disciples that involve closely personal beliefs and attitudes. It is almost a sort of spiritual program, and has affinities with the discourse on behavior in the community in Matthew 18.

Scandals

FIRST, A REFLECTION on scandals in the community. The way the word "scandal" has developed is itself a commentary on human nature. In current usage it means something disgraceful and much talked about, a subject of gossip: "That couple's behavior is a public scandal." The commentary on human nature is that regrettably most of us enjoy talking about the major failures of others (not our friends), and broadcasting them to anyone who has been unfortunate enough to miss them. The original meaning of "scandal" is, however, importantly different. It is an obstacle such as a stone in the way, a catch or a trip wire, which causes someone to fall over. In this sense my example may be a scandal to a single person without becoming at all public knowledge. Even a quiet suggestion will do, or anything that leads another to fail or defect from Christian behavior. "Little ones" is a standard Gospel expression for the helpless and vulnerable, which explains why the dire and irretrievable punishment of the millstone is appropriate.

Forgiveness

IN MATTHEW 18, the chapter on relationships within the community, it is taken for granted that there will be offenses and hurts. Such is the stuff of human beings living and working together. What is specific about the Christian community is not that these do not occur, but that efforts are to be made to mend them, heal them, and put them right. It is far easier to write off an offensive or hurtful colleague—often with a certain pleasurable conviction that he or she will get a millstone around the neck in the end—than to set about mending the breach. Correction will require thought, tact, and timing, and certainly forgiveness in the heart. Correction and criticism administered in anger may often benefit through the home truths blurted out, but will hardly heal the wounds of community. Matthew has a whole succession of legal processes about correction within the community. Luke is more informal, merely linking it closely to forgiveness.

Similarly with forgiveness itself: Matthew, thinking more of formal structure in the community, gives the question about forgiveness to Peter, and so links forgiveness to authority in the community. Luke again leaves it more informal. In Matthew, Jesus demands forgiveness seventy times seven, in Luke only seven times, but seven times daily. There can be no limit to forgiveness. It is anybody's calculation which of the two is the more demanding, but in any case the number seven denotes perfection.

Faith

THERE IS A double confusion over the form of this saying. Matthew 17:20 has "If your faith *is* . . . you *will* say," a provision for the future. Luke gives the muddled "If you *had* faith . . . you *could* say," which leaves it unclear whether the disciples are presumed to have faith or not. The second confusion is over the mulberry tree: The original saying in Mark 11 concerns the transfer of a mountain into the sea, but occurs after the withering of the fig tree. Luke by confused reminiscence has a mulberry tree transferred into the sea, where it would hardly flourish! The confusion shows the importance of the saying and its frequent use. It must have been handed down and repeated widely in the oral tradition before it came into fixed and written form.

The content of the faith is not detailed. If the saying comes from the pre-Easter Jesus, as it does in the Marcan and Matthean stories, it cannot concern resurrection faith. It must mean more generally concentration upon, trust in, reliance on Jesus as bringing God to us. This indeed is the foundation of all Christian living.

PRAYER
Lord, I believe. Help my unbelief! (Mark 9:24, RSV)

TWO STORIES ABOUT GRATITUDE

The Servant's Wages

THIS FORCEFUL PARABLE of the useless servants can seem surprising after the praise of service that has been such a feature of Jesus' message. The Son of Man came not to be served but to serve, and the dignity of the Christian consists in echoing that service. How does the parable square with "Blessed are those servants whom the master finds awake when he comes. In truth I tell you, he will do up his belt, sit them down at table, and wait on them" (12:37)? There is no real contradiction. The point being made is that it is impossible to earn favors or gratitude from God. Everything God gives is pure gift, an unearned blessing, from the favor bestowed on Mary onward. The servants of God have no rights and can have no complaints. Matthew teaches the same hard lesson with his parable of the payment of the vineyard workers, which seems so unfair. No human being can enter into reckoning with God. So, if any reader feels inclined to say "Behave like this and you won't get far in today's labor market," that reflection is itself quite important. You can't sue God or quote contracts of employment at him. God is not in today's labor market. There can be only gratitude on our part, and gratitude all flows in the other direction.

The Ten Lepers

THE STORY OF ten lepers is unique to Luke, without parallel in Mark or Matthew. In style and language it is typical of Luke. It has two features that are favorites with Luke—Samaritans and gratitude to God. As in the story of the good Samaritan, Samaritans in Luke represent non-Jews who are open to the message of Jesus and respond to his call. All the ten lepers show faith in Jesus. They call him "Master!" They have so much faith that they start to go off to show themselves to the priests to record their cure before it has even occurred; they were already on the way when they found themselves cured. But there the praiseworthy behavior of the other nine ceases; in their joy and relief they simply go off and neglect him whom they have so recently called "Master." Presumably the other nine cured lepers were Jews, so that there is a deliberate contrast in their behavior: This Samaritan, the only beneficiary to show a response to Jesus' action, is the forerunner of the Gentiles who will enter the Christian community in the Acts.

It is a strange thing that human gratitude as such is expressed in the Gospels hardly at all. The normal word for "thanks" appears only in the story previous to this, of the master who does not thank his slave. The more formal word for "thanks," used for the eucharist, occurs outside a eucharistic context only in Luke. But there is plenty of its equivalent in Luke, for it is Luke especially who shows us people praising or glorifying God in gratitude after a miracle; this imparts an air of cheerfulness and celebration to the whole Gospel. This praise starts as soon as Jesus is born, the angels, then the shepherds praising God (2:13, 20). The joyful canticles of Zechariah, Mary, and Simeon are perfect expressions of their gratitude and recognition of God's gifts. Praise and delight are often the natural expression of thanks, as one sees in a child delighted with a present, who shows it off with enthusiasm to anyone on the scene, praising the giver of the present. Just as, in another story, the healed paralytic goes off home praising God, with a joy that spreads to the onlookers (5:25–26). The healed Gerasene demoniac "proclaimed throughout the city all that Jesus had done for him" (8:39). This becomes so regular after the miracles that the curmudgeonly "other nine" in this story are rather the exception than the rule, though the racket made by the Samaritan does seem to be exceptional!

PRAYER

Lord, I need to know my position. You owe me no thanks and I owe you infinite thanks. Let me enumerate just some of the things for which I need to thank you (life, health, intelligence, movement, love, your friendship, eternal life) and give you joyful praise for your generosity.

THE DAY OF THE SON OF MAN

The Earliest Christian Hopes

POSSIBLY THE MOST pressing question of all left by Jesus' proclamation of the kingdom/kingship of God was "When?" Had it come already? Would it come soon? What part in it did the death and resurrection of Jesus play? Mark, followed by Matthew, had concluded the account of Jesus' ministry with an extended discourse by Jesus on the future of his followers. Mark 13 ends with a promise that the Son of Man will come on the clouds of heaven to gather his chosen ones. Matthew 24–25 includes the same, and ends with the great scene of the last judgment.

Both these Gospel writers show just how vivid was the expectation of the coming of Jesus in triumph to take his followers with him in his victory procession, an expectation shared by Paul in his early letters to the Thessalonians and the Corinthians. Luke must have written some years after this. The expected coming simply had not happened, so his perspective and his message are entirely different.

All Around You

THE PHARISEES OPEN the discussion with one of those useful Lucan foil questions, simply a hook on which to hang the answer: "The coming of the kingdom of God does not admit of observation . . . the kingdom of God is among you." These two elements will be developed, so it is important to understand them. The word translated "observation" is used only here in the New Testament, but it must have recalled Exodus 12:42, where it was used to describe the vigil of the Passover night. But it is no use keeping vigil, watching for the kingdom to come. On the contrary, the kingdom is all around you. Luke does not mean that the kingdom is hidden in individual hearts. He means, as his stress on the ideal community of the church in the Acts shows, that the kingdom is all around you in the community. Our task is not to keep vigil and watch for the coming of the kingdom, but it is to further God's kingdom in our daily lives.

The remainder of Jesus' explanation expands on this point. Looking for visible manifestations of the kingdom can be discouraging, even a distraction: However much you long to see, you will not do so. Quite possibly Luke is stressing the point because Christians saw various historical events, such as the destruction of Jerusalem in A.D. 70, as moments of the coming of the kingdom, when what is all-important is the life of the Christian community.

He is determined also to prevent Christians from becoming engrossed in the preoccupations of the world. So he repeatedly stresses that when the moment does come, it will be sudden and dire for those who are engrossed in the pleasures of eating and drinking, the preoccupations of marrying, and business interests such as marketing, agriculture, and construction. He uses the stock Old Testament examples of destructive judgment, namely the eras of Noah and Lot. Destruction then was sudden and unpredictable: There was no warning of the flood, nor of the engulfing of Sodom and Gomorrah. There will be no possibility of salvaging anything, as the dire consequences of even the backward glance of Lot's wife showed.

The End of the World?

TO MANY CHRISTIANS today, any idea of the end of the world is as meaningless as a literal understanding of stars falling from heaven and the Son of Man coming on the clouds. It is a piece of imagery culled from the Hebrew prescientific world view, which must now be discarded. But the gospel message expressed in these terms cannot be disregarded. At the very least, it is a proclamation, enshrined in ancient imagery, that there is a forward thrust to history, and at the end of history (personal or cosmic?) an account must be given. The perils of absorption in the pleasures and affairs of human life, to the detriment of concern for the kingdom, remain as real as ever.

PRAYER
Lord God, whatever your plans for the world and its completion,
help me to keep working for the fulfillment of your kingship. Do not let
me become engulfed in the attractions of life, but keep always your
values and your vision clear in my sight.

TWO PARABLES ON PRAYER

The Unjust Judge

THIS IS A typical Lucan parable, teaching perseverance in prayer. There is the little monologue by the chief character, reflecting on how to get out of his difficult situation, just like the rich fool or the crafty steward. Only in Luke is the chief character of parables a rogue, unjust but with a certain pragmatic realism that makes him not unattractive. And only Luke has these parables that do not so much illustrate the situation as encourage to a particular kind of action.

Just as it is possible and attractive to see the parable of the rich fool as taking up a hint in the book of Ecclesiasticus, so we are drawn to see this parable as a mirror image of the earlier sketch of a fair-minded judge in the same book:

> *He does not ignore the orphan's supplication,*
> *nor the widow's as she pours out her complaint.*
> *Do the widow's tears not run down her cheeks,*
> *as she accuses the man who is the cause of them? (35:14–15)*

In both passages there are the widow and the judge, and in both the widow wins by her perseverance in her plea. But in Luke the judge is represented almost as the personification of injustice, for throughout the biblical tradition "orphans and widows" are the personification of helpless vulnerability, to protect who must be the first object of any system of justice. In addition, Luke has remolded the judge to be one of his own lively characters. This is the more audacious because he makes the person whom one is tempted to allegorize as God into a mixed character who does the right thing for the wrong reason. Another delightfully brazen touch of realism in the judge's ruthless assessment of his self-interest is the risk from the widow: This is often translated as if she will come and "outface" him or "pester him"; in fact, the normal meaning of the word is "hit in the face." She will come and give him a clip on the ear or a black eye!

The Day of the Lord

THE TAILPIECE OF this parable about perseverance in prayer attaches it to the important previous scenario of the day of the Son of Man, which will finally come so suddenly. It is almost as though Luke, having noted that nothing was said about prayer in that section, decided to tack this on. During the time of the Church, and the persecutions that go with it, persevering prayer will be vital.

The Pharisee and the Tax Collector

NOT ONLY PERSEVERANCE but the right attitude in prayer will be vital. Tax collectors like Zacchaeus are by nature outcasts, so the object of Luke's special attention: No matter how roguish they are, all sinners need to do in order to win acceptance is repent, like the prodigal son, to acknowledge their fault and turn to the Lord. This is precisely the point of difference between the two characters, as in the prodigal son. As in that story, but more simply, the characters are painted with deft touches, the simple, contrite tax collector and the oily, complacent Pharisee. Luke even dares to say that he prays "to himself" rather than to God; no doubt one could understand this as meaning sotto voce, but the double meaning is there! He may have raised his eyes piously to heaven, but Luke does venture to give the tactful hint that he can also spare a sidelong glance at "this tax collector here." The delicious irony of the Pharisee's prayer is that we all know it to be humbug. Throughout the Gospel the Pharisees have been presented precisely as avaricious, unjust, an "adulterous generation," and hypocritical about their fasting and tithing.

That Luke is not necessarily wide of the mark is shown by Rabbi Nechonias' unfortunate prayer (about A.D. 70): "I thank you, Lord my God, that you have set my lot among those who frequent the synagogue rather than those who sit on street corners. I run my course for the life of the world to come, while they are heading for the abyss." There seems nothing left to ask for.

All this contrasts with the straightforward, genuine directness of the tax collector's prayer, the perfect example of simplicity and repentance.

PRAYER
God, be merciful to me, a sinner.

TWO APPROACHES TO JESUS

AT THIS POINT in the travel narrative Luke rejoins the narrative of Mark and Matthew with two fiercely contrasting stories.

The Little Children

EACH OF THE evangelists has his own lesson to tell in this story. Mark's story is a picture of Jesus' humanity, gentleness, and open welcome. He is angry with the disciples for trying to send the children away, and, to make the point of his warmth even clearer, embraces the children and lays his hands upon them. For Matthew it is a lesson in conversion. He inserts "whoever does not *change and become* like little children," so it is a matter of the spiritual dispositions of children. Rather than any such imagined quality as the innocence or guilelessness of children, he must mean the openness and simplicity of children before the Father in heaven.

Luke has yet another lesson. There is no interest in the spiritual qualities of the candidate for the kingdom, for he says they "even brought babies to him," using a word that indicates a newborn babe. His interest, therefore, is in the helplessness of the candidate; the candidate can contribute nothing at all. No one can earn entry into the kingdom. This passage, then, joins those that surround it: in the previous passage the tax collector in prayer can only plead his lack of qualities and his guilt. In the following passage we are told that no human being can earn entry into the kingdom.

The Rich Ruler

FOR THIS PASSAGE Luke uses Mark's story, but by the smallest changes makes its message uncompromisingly severe. In Mark it is a warm, vibrant scene: The man shows his eagerness and good intentions by coming running up to Jesus and doing him reverence. Jesus responds with affection; he "looks at him and loves him" (NIV); and, although the man chokes (the normal meaning of the Greek word) over the requirement to sell what he has, he goes away sad. Matthew makes the scene more touching still by calling him a "young man" and by removing the slight wariness of Jesus at being called "good."

But Luke hardens the scene. There is no sign of youth, and little of eagerness. No running up, no reverence, merely a question, possibly hostile or, at any rate, distant. The man has become "one of the rulers," a magistrate or perhaps a president of the synagogue. Perhaps this is to accommodate him to Luke's own more distinguished audience—the Gospel is addressed to "your Excellency" Theophilus—or perhaps to link him to those who had been habitually opposing Jesus. It puts him from the beginning on the side of the Pharisee rather than on the side of the tax collector. Correspondingly, there is no sign of affection from Jesus. His demands are more absolute or even unyielding. He insists that the ruler sell "*everything* you own" (imitating the disciples, all of whom in Luke leave *everything* when they come to follow Jesus) and not merely give, but *distribute* it, scatter it abroad, among the poor. Then, although the ruler does have the decency to be "overcome with sadness," Luke does not let him go away, but keeps him there to hear Jesus' virtual condemnation of his position. Now we see why he has encountered such hard treatment: He not merely has many possessions as in Mark; he is exceedingly wealthy—one might almost say "stinking rich."

The Eye of the Needle

THE FINAL CHANGE in Luke is perhaps the most important. Not only does he keep the wealthy ruler onstage; instead of addressing the disciples alone, all reference to the immediate audience is removed, and Jesus addresses the whole message to the ruler and to everyone else without distinction. It is an uncompromising message. There is no escape in the old legend that by "the eye of the needle" Jesus means a small gate in Jerusalem; no such gate is known to have existed. It is the same sort of uncompromising statement as that only those who "hate" their dearest relatives can enter the kingdom. Wealth is a positive bar, and only through the power of God can any be saved.

PRAYER

May I realize, Lord, how helpless I am. I can only put obstacles in your way, never earn your kingdom. Help me at least to sweep away the obstacles.

A PROPHECY OF THE PASSION

As JESUS AND his disciples approach Jerusalem comes this almost ago-
nizing moment of the prophecy of the Passion, which the disciples fail to
understand.

The Three Prophecies in Mark

THIS PROPHECY MUST be seen against the background of Mark's three
formal prophecies of the Passion. Mark stakes out the second half of his
Gospel, starting immediately after Peter's confession at Caesarea Philippi,
by Jesus' three prophecies of his Passion, the reiteration becoming ever
more explicit and ever more painful. Each time the disciples fail to understand, and indeed show their disregard by squabbling about their own
position and precedence. Luke has only this single prophecy, but the
threat of the coming Passion looms just as dominantly through the theme
of the great journey to Jerusalem, an ever-present reality, ever since Jesus,
Moses, and Elijah are seen conversing about it at the transfiguration. Luke
does not, then, repeat the prophecy three times, but the emphasis on the
inability of the disciples to understand is nevertheless heavy, expressed
with three dull thuds in the single verse 34.

The Scandal of the Cross

FAMILIARITY WITH THE Christian symbol of the cross has blunted our
perception of the shocking nature of this event. It was a punishment
refined by the Romans and reserved for slaves. After the preliminaries,
which could be more or less brutal, the victim was simply nailed up naked
and left to die, exposed both to the unforgiving heat of the sun and the
insults and contempt of passersby. Crucifixion took place normally beside
a road for maximum publicity. After the major slave revolts of Rome, the
approach roads were lined with thousands of dead and dying bodies, hang-
ing there. Jesus was crucified beside the main road from Jerusalem to the
coast. The brutality of the business may be judged from the fact that

during the siege of Jerusalem in A.D. 70 the Roman besiegers nailed any escapees to the trees of the Mount of Olives till there were none left free. They amused themselves by nailing them up in odd positions. Even the orator Cicero, not the most squeamish of Romans, describes crucifixion as a most disgusting punishment.

In the first two centuries of Christianity, while the memory of crucifixion still lingered, realistic images of Jesus crucified were never attempted. Instead, the cross was represented bejeweled, to show the glorification of the cross. It is hardly surprising that the crucified Christ was "to the Jews an obstacle they cannot get over, to the Gentiles foolishness" (1 Corinthians 1:23).

Why Crucifixion?

THIS FOOLISHNESS AND disgrace must, therefore, be explained. Two avenues of explanation are used here, firstly that Jesus knew about it beforehand and went willingly, indeed voluntarily, to this death, and secondly that it was destined by the will of God, expressed in the scriptures. Luke especially insists that "it was necessary" that Jesus should suffer, and that each move toward the crucifixion was destined to take place. Thus now Jesus describes in detail the events of his Passion, exactly as they would occur.

It is likely that the details of the prophecy were clarified after the event. How much did Jesus know? He must have known that his proclamation of the kingship of God had set him on a collision course with the authorities at Jerusalem, and that they would not be able to tolerate his message. He must also have known that his Father would not desert him. On the other hand, it is hard to believe that the disciples, having heard three detailed descriptions of the Passion and resurrection, still reacted not only with cowardice but also with surprise when it actually occurred. The detailing of the events is a way of showing that Jesus knew just what he was doing, and willingly accepted the consequences.

PRAYER
Lord Jesus, you knew beforehand that you were to be brutally rejected, and yet you still carried through your mission. Grant me courage to carry on in difficulties, and trust in your saving help.

JESUS HEALS BARTIMAEUS

AFTER THIS OMINOUS prophecy of the Passion the air is full of the threat of the coming events. Jericho is the first place apart from Jerusalem to be mentioned since Samaria in 17:11. It is the obvious last place before Jerusalem, less than a day's walk from the city up the Wadi Qilt, which featured in the story of the good Samaritan. This serves as a reminder of how close the city now is, a sort of prelude to Jesus' arrival. In order to locate the following story of Zacchaeus in Jericho, Luke changes the location of the Bartimaeus incident, putting it at Jesus' entrance to Jericho instead of when Jesus is leaving the town. This is the last of Jesus' miracles of healing.

Son of David

THIS IS THE first time in Luke that Jesus has been hailed as Son of David. At the annunciation Mary had been told that Jesus would inherit the throne of his father David, and another reminder was given by his birth at Bethlehem, the city of David. Since then, his descent from David has never been mentioned. Perhaps this Jewish title was of less interest to Luke's Gentile audience. In the story of Jesus as told by the other Synoptic evangelists, however, it has an important role as a messianic title, for the royal Messiah was to be son of David. There are constant messianic overtones to Jesus' ministry, simply through his proclamation of the kingship of God through his miracles and his teaching. Nevertheless, Jesus would not allow his disciples to proclaim him as Messiah, "until after the Son of Man had risen from the dead" (Mark 9:9). This was because they were so slow to understand the real nature of his mission.

There were in Judaism many different hopes and expectations current about the Messiah. He would bring the sovereignty of God to perfection, but how? Would he be a warlord who would free Israel from the Roman yoke? Would he bring fire and judgment to the world, separating the wheat from the chaff? Would he ensure that the Law of God was observed to the last jot and tittle? Would he bring abundance and plenty to enable every man to luxuriate in milk and honey under his own fig tree? That he would bring God's sovereignty to perfection by his own suffering and death was never part of the conception of the Messiah. That would involve the rejection of God's Messiah by God's own people, their failure to recognize the fulfillment of the promises for which they had waited so long, and this could surely not even be envisaged. The disciples, too, were slow to appreciate what was the nature of Jesus' messiahship. So Jesus was hesitant about the use of the title of Messiah, until the real nature of his mission would be forced upon them by its climax and conclusion.

Within this pattern it is significant that now at last Jesus is finally hailed publicly as "Son of David," just as he is physically going up the last ascent to Jerusalem, where the nature of his messiahship will be made known by the Passion and resurrection. Now at last he makes no move to silence Bartimaeus, and surely accepts his cry of "Son of David!" as an expression of the faith that saves him.

Bartimaeus

AT THIS STAGE, therefore, the miracle of opening the eyes of the blind has special significance. It symbolizes the opening of the eyes of understanding that is about to take place with the revelation of the suffering Messiah at Jerusalem. It also somehow has the air of a special celebration, summing up Jesus' miracles of healing. So many features of previous miracles are present here too. There is the persistence in prayer shown by Bartimaeus' repeated cry, despite the scolding of those who heard him. Luke also stresses his helplessness: In Mark, as soon as Jesus tells the bystanders to call Bartimaeus to him, Bartimaeus flings off his cloak, leaps up, and comes to Jesus; in Luke's account he has to be led to Jesus. The only contribution he makes himself is faith, the acknowledgment that Jesus has power to save him (and "save" is again used in an unrestricted sense, suggesting not merely the restoration of sight, but the saving of the whole person). Finally there is that characteristically Lucan outburst of joyful thanks and praise to God by the whole people of God present.

PRAYER
Son of David, have pity on me!

ZACCHAEUS

AS THE STORY of Bartimaeus sums up Jesus' miracles of healing, so the story of Zacchaeus sums up the welcome Jesus gives to sinners. The story comes only in Luke, and two interesting balancing stories have been suggested for it. Particularly telling are Jesus' two final sayings, firstly that even Zacchaeus, the despised tax collector, is a son of Abraham. This takes us right back to John the Baptist's message of repentance: To the claim of his listeners that they were anyway children of Abraham, John replies that God can raise up children of Abraham from these very stones. Now even the rankest outcast is seen to be granted this status by his repentance. Secondly, it is another instance of Jesus coming to save what was lost, which has been stressed so heavily in the three parables of the lost sheep, the lost coin, and the lost son. Now Jesus voices the principle in terms reminiscent of that early saying, "It is not those that are well who need the doctor, but the sick" (5:31).

The story is told with typical Lucan zest. The scene is set, with Jesus going peacefully through Jericho, that wonderfully fertile city of palm trees, deliciously irrigated by the Spring of Elisha (2 Kings 2:19–22), the first known site of agriculture and the oldest city in the world (it has a stone tower some 8,000 years old). Zacchaeus himself has that mild eccentricity that is the mark of many of Luke's characters: It is not every head tax collector who would shin up the nearest sycamore tree, just as not every master would congratulate his crafty steward on cheating him out of his money. The lack of regard for his dignity partners the same lack of care for appearances in the father of the prodigal son. One never quite knows what Luke's characters will get up to next. Jesus, needless to say, is not the least fazed by seeing this dignified character clinging to the branches. The lively dialogue is also a feature of Luke's stories.

The generosity of Zacchaeus' little speech remains in character: He is, after all, a financier and used to dealing with figures, so is exact about them. He does not promise to make himself destitute, but promises to give a neat half of his goods to the poor. Is this the scale of donation we are to consider ideal from the rich to the poor? The disciples when they are called forsake "everything." But in the Acts Ananias and Sapphira incur their dire penalty not for holding something back but for lying to the Spirit about having done so (Acts 5:3). The fourfold restitution to those he has wronged is also generous, for the Law demanded that "the person must restore in full the amount owed, with one-fifth added" (Numbers 5:7). Zacchaeus' promise goes far beyond this.

But, of course, the most important feature is the repentance of the chief tax collector. Tax collectors, as we have often seen, were notoriously outcasts from decent religious society because they were working for the Romans, playing a part in their oppression of the Jews; but this is the first time we have met one of their leaders, who would earn an intensification of that hate and contempt.

Parallels

LUKE MAY ALSO intend us to see in this story of the repentance of a sinner a balance with another sinner, the woman who wept on Jesus' feet at the house of Simon in Luke 7:36–50. This would be in accordance with Luke's careful pairing of men and women: Both are sinners who welcome and embrace Jesus in repentance.

On the other hand, there is also perhaps a contrast between Zacchaeus and the rich ruler of Luke 18:15–30 (see no. 64). Both are described by the same word as "wealthy." Both are men of position, the one an *archon* (ruler), the other an *architelones* (chief tax collector). There the similarity ends and the contrast begins, for Zacchaeus responds where the rich ruler fails. The rich ruler is held back by his wealth from following Jesus, and cannot face distributing his goods to the poor. Zacchaeus does precisely this to repair his previous injustice.

PRAYER

Lord, I suppose we, each of us, have something of which we are ashamed, which would make us outcasts from your company. Grant me profound repentance, a real turning back to you from sin, and an adherence to you, that I too may be a child of Abraham.

THE PARABLE OF THE POUNDS

THIS FINAL PARABLE story is often read in the light of the parallel story in Matthew. Matthew has the parable of the talents as one of his five parable stories about the impending last judgment. Luke's story is commonly seen as a version of the same story, with a few variations. For instance, the sums of money are less gigantic. It is difficult to give equivalents of ancient monetary values in an age when there were no cars, washing machines, or holidays to the Bahamas to buy, but Matthew's talent is equivalent to the annual tribute paid by a small province of the empire to Rome, so a gigantic sum, whereas Luke's *mna* (often translated "pound") is more like half a year's wages for an agricultural worker. A second obvious difference is that Luke includes the dimension that the master is not simply a man going on a business trip or on vacation, but is a nobleman going to secure a kingdom. The historical allusion is surely to King Herod's son Archelaus, who went to Rome to secure the kingdom of Judea, which he did successfully despite an embassy of the Jews that followed him to prevent it (they were quite right, and he was so incompetent that he was deposed after ten years in A.D. 6). The question is whether this historical background is merely a literary decoration, or whether it is the whole point that has transformed the story.

The importance of the political dimension in the story itself may be gauged from two factors: The successful servants are given charge not of more money but of cities; that is, they participate in the new king's rule. Furthermore, the final incident in the story is the punishment, not of the timid servant but of the objectors, who are slaughtered forthwith. Some weight must also be given to the introduction to the story, which gives the reason for the parable as that "they thought that the kingdom of God was going to show itself then and there"; so, somehow or other, the kingdom should be central.

The Return of the King

THE WHOLE QUESTION is when the king is reckoned to gain his kingdom. Is it at the end of the world? In this case the parable is a warning to use one's abilities to good advantage in view of the final judgment, a warning against the final judgment, much like Matthew's parable. On the other hand, the special features of the story answer better to a different scenario: The moment when Jesus receives his kingdom is at the Passion and resurrection. This is already indicated in the introduction: They thought that the kingdom of God was going to show itself then and there. From then on in the Gospel story the emphasis is on the achievement of the kingdom, at the entry into Jerusalem and on the cross as well as at the resurrection. After this he will give apostolic authority in the Christian community to those who are faithful. This corresponds to the authority of the good servants over ten or five cities. The servant who merely wrapped his money in a cloth is not (as in Matthew's story) punished; he merely has his money taken away and is not given authority. The corresponding authority is given to others. The punishment falls on those who wanted the kingdom denied to this king, and they are surely the leaders of the Jews.

Luke's scheme of history has two parts: After the life of Jesus, climaxing in his death and resurrection, his mission is carried on by his apostles in the power of the Spirit, as described in the second volume of Luke's history, the Acts of the Apostles. There is, so to speak, a second chance, and many of the Jews take it and are converted to Christianity. But the leaders still reject it, and they are the "enemies" who would not have the king rule over them.

It must be admitted that there are still puzzling features in the story. Why does the timid slave accuse the king of being so exacting, a charge the king accepts? And what is the point of the protest of the bystanders?

PRAYER

Lord, banish laziness, slackness, and lack of interest from me.
Make me aware of what I can do for your kingdom, of the tasks you
have entrusted to me, and help me to respond wholeheartedly to
your offer.

JESUS' ROYAL ENTRY INTO JERUSALEM

JESUS' ENTRY INTO Jerusalem is a point of high significance. It is already so in Mark, but in Luke this significance is further heightened by the previous story. The long and single-minded journey to Jerusalem since 9:51 has focused attention on this moment. The parable immediately preceding this one, about journeying to receive the royal dignity, has especially prepared for this event. Hardly any other place-name has intruded into the story (Samaria once, and Jericho), and now at the end it is reinforced that he is "going up to Jerusalem" (19:28).

The Preparations

THE STORY OF the acquisition of the colt is full of mystery, a supreme example of the authority of Jesus. We are not told of any preparation for this, such as that the owners of the colt knew Jesus or had been warned. They simply yield unquestioningly when they are told, "The Lord has need of it" (RSV). The mystery is intensified in that neither they nor the reader know who this "Lord" is. The word used can mean either "the master" in the sense of an earthly owner or (as frequently in Luke) the Lord God. This ambiguity is surely deliberate. The fact that it is important that no one has yet ridden the colt is a further hint of the sacredness of the moment, for it indicates that the mount, like a sacred sacrificial victim, had never been subjected to any common use.

The solemnity of the occasion is increased by two scriptural allusions that would spring immediately to mind. Entry riding on such a colt is the fulfillment of the prophecy in Zechariah 9:9 of the king who comes in peace: "Look, your king is approaching . . . humble and riding on a donkey, on a colt, the foal of a donkey." This motif of peace is stressed twice more in the story, by the cries of those who welcomed him (v. 38) and by Jesus himself in his lament (v. 42). His entry into Jerusalem was meant not to condemn but to save Jerusalem—if the city had been open to this. The second allusion is even more portentous: By his mention of the descent of the Mount of Olives (v. 37) Luke reminds the reader of the awesome scene of Zechariah 14, the Day of the Lord, when the Lord comes to Jerusalem with all his holy ones from the Mount of Olives.

The Entry

THE ACTUAL HISTORICAL scene could have been quite simple. It was not necessarily a grand triumphal procession that any onlooker would have recognized as Jesus' royal entry. Pilgrims went up for the great feasts such as the Dedication of the Temple singing Psalm 118 and waving palm branches. There would have been great crowds by the time they came to the gates of Jerusalem. Neither Mark nor Luke indicate in fact a massive retinue: Mark has only "those who went in front and those who followed" (how many were they?), and Luke's "the whole group of disciples" gives no indication of number. So the significance of their entry among the pilgrims—though nonetheless real—may have been seen only later, when the disciples looked back on the events.

There are some little touches by which Luke shows his understanding of the meaning of the event. First, they kept strewing their cloaks under him as he went forward, which is reminiscent of the acclaim of Jehu as king in 2 Kings 9:13; this they did, crying "Jehu is king." Luke also stresses the kingship of Jesus by a slight adjustment to the psalm, the addition of the word "the king." They cry, "Blessed is he who is coming *as king* in the name of the Lord." In Mark it is only after the psalm verse that "the coming kingdom of David our father" is mentioned.

A final adjustment made by Luke to the entry is the touching echo of the song of the angels at Bethlehem. "Peace in heaven and glory in the highest heavens" echoes "Glory to God in the highest heaven, and on earth peace for those he favors," but with a tragic difference: Despite Luke's contant emphasis that Jesus' message is "the gospel of peace," "the word of peace," there is no promise here that Jesus' entry will in fact bring peace to Jerusalem.

PRAYER
Blessed is he who is coming as king in the name of the Lord.
Peace in heaven and glory in the highest.

LAMENT OVER JERUSALEM

THE SADNESS OF Jesus at Jerusalem's refusal to accept him is a recurrent theme in Luke. We have seen it already at the halfway point of the great journey (13:34–35, no. 53 in this book). It will recur again in the reply to the women who mourn for Jesus on the way to execution (23:28–31). Perhaps the most tragic feature is the echo and reversal of the *Benedictus*. Zechariah had foretold the salvation of Israel in similar terms. Israel would be saved "from our *enemies*" (1:71, 74) when God comes "to visit us, . . . to guide our feet into the *way of peace*" (1:78–79). But instead, Jerusalem fails to recognize the visitation from on high and so the *way to peace* (19:42). Consequently it will be the *enemies* who surround her (19:43) and besiege her.

The Siege of Jerusalem

A QUESTION, OF course, immediately arises, whether, in the words of Jesus' prophecy on this occasion, Luke is making use of his knowledge of the siege of Jerusalem some forty years later. It is certainly not impossible or unacceptable in theory that Luke should have clarified the words by his knowledge of what actually happened. This would give valuable clues to the date of writing of the Gospel. In fact, this avenue is disappointingly closed. None of the Gospel mentions of the fate of Jerusalem contains details that need to be culled from what eventually happened. The details of the siege are given by Josephus at some length, and none of them is clearly reflected in the Gospel passages. It was the concern of the Gospel writers far more to show the theological import of the sack of Jerusalem, that the fate of Jerusalem was the fulfillment not only of Jesus' prophecies but also the prophecies of the Old Testament. So the fate of Jerusalem is described in the stock prophetic language used by the prophets to describe the sack of any town. For instance, there was not a fortification built all around Jerusalem (this would have taxed even the Romans' skill in engineering), and the dashing of "children inside your walls to the ground" is a clear reminiscence of Psalm 137:9.

Jerusalem and the Jews in the Gospel of Luke

THE GREAT DIFFICULTY for Luke, as for Paul, was to explain how it was that the promises of God to his Chosen People had been fulfilled. How was it that the Jews as a whole had not accepted Christ, but had rejected the fulfillment of their national hopes? Had God forgotten or deserted his people? Both writers were concerned chiefly with Christians sprung from non-Jewish stock, but they both toiled over the mysterious failure of the Jews, how it was that the focus of Christianity had moved from the Jews to the Gentiles, and what the status of the Jews now was.

It is against this background that Luke's attitude to the Jews must be seen. In the infancy narratives he stresses strongly that John the Baptist and Jesus are the fulfillment precisely of Jewish hopes: The parents of both children are models of Jewish piety, perfect examples of the poor and helpless favored by the God of Israel. Jesus, in his opening sermon at Nazareth, shows that he has come to fulfill the prophecies. Throughout the Gospel a clear distinction is made between the people and their leaders. The former are responsive to Jesus and are treated sympathetically, the latter unfavorable and heavily criticized. Later, in the Acts of the Apostles, Luke is at pains to point out that always some of the Jews responded to the message of Christ and were converted, despite the continued opposition of their leaders. The first Christian community at Jerusalem is represented as the ideal community, marked by prayer, fraternity, and harmony.

It is as part of this presentation that Jerusalem features in the Gospel. The Gospel begins in Jerusalem, and the pilgrimage to the climax at Jerusalem occupies the latter part of the Gospel. It is the scene of the resurrection appearances. It is the hinge point from which the Gospel spreads all over the known world. In the course of his journeys Paul is constantly returning there to confirm his message.

At the midpoint of the story, therefore, the final phase of Jesus' ministry, Jesus himself comes to Jerusalem. It should have been the hinge of all his mission, the enthusiastic center and promoter of his work. Its failure to respond is a large part of the tragedy of Jesus.

Prayer

Lord, I am your favored child, just as the Jews were, chosen and fostered through all time. Grant that I may respond to your call and follow you in the road of my peace.

JESUS IN THE TEMPLE

THIS IS A passage where the full impact of Luke's message can be seen only by comparison to the account given by the other evangelists; there are staggering differences in the account of these events. Luke's is not simply an abbreviated account; it is a radically different one.

The Purging of the Temple

MARK'S ACCOUNT OF the "purging of the temple" is a statement of the bankruptcy of Judaism. In a prophetic action Jesus "rubbishes" the temple, upsetting those who did business there and finally declaring it a "den of thieves." In itself this was only a symbolic action. It is impossible to believe that Jesus raged in the temple, creating widespread havoc, for a close watch for disturbances was kept not only by the temple police but by the Roman guard as well. He would have been arrested before he got very far. The meaning of this demonstration is given by Mark through the little story of the cursing of the fig tree. Mark often "sandwiches" one event between two halves of another in order that they may react on and interpret one another. In this case the fig tree obviously stands for Israel, so that its barrenness is a sign of the barrenness of Israel.

Furthermore, the prominence of Jesus' word against the temple, "Destroy this temple and in three days I will rebuild it," in the Passion narrative confirms that Jesus' hostile attitude to and threat against the temple were the real reasons the leaders of the Jews wanted him removed from the scene. He had caused upset in the temple once, and the chief priests and Sadducees were not prepared to risk it happening again, particularly at the big feast of Passover, when the whole of Jerusalem would be thronged with pilgrims. As the high priest so succinctly indicates, if this happened, the Romans would come and take away their power on the grounds that they were incompetent to control the people. What made it worse was Jesus' link with John the Baptist, who was still reverenced by the people.

Luke and Jesus the Teacher in the Temple

LUKE TRANSFORMS THIS scene. Instead of Jesus taking action on four different groups of people, those buying, selling, changing money, and selling doves (Mark 11:15–16), in Luke he merely begins driving out those who were selling. This is merely a preliminary, and the accent is on their replacement: "He taught in the temple every day." He clears out the sellers in order that he may teach, and day after day. The full extent of this is seen at the end of Jesus' ministry in Jerusalem: "All day long he would be in the temple teaching . . . and from early morning the people thronged to him in the temple to listen to him" (21:37–38). These two statements form a bracket around Jesus' Jerusalem activity, emphasizing his continuous teaching office; his messianic teaching is the core of his activity in Jerusalem. He makes the temple his regular platform.

Significantly, however, Luke also abbreviates the scriptural quotation from Isaiah given by Mark, "My house will be called a house of prayer for all peoples." By removing the final three words, "for all peoples," Luke deletes the suggestion of the destined inclusion of the Gentiles. For Luke the temple serves as the center of teaching for Jesus and of prayer for the early Christian community of Jerusalem, but thereafter its usefulness is at an end. Stephen's great speech in Acts 7 against the temple signals its end as a sacred sphere. It is no longer the center of prayer and true worship.

The Beginning of the End

THIS SCENE CONSTITUTES the spark that ignites the fire of determination to get rid of Jesus. The chief priests and the lawyers burn to get rid of him, in marked contrast to the people (and Luke twice uses the word *laos*, which designates the sacred People of God), who hung on his words. The chief priests were the principal authorities in the temple, and also largely the secular powers in Jerusalem. In Luke the cause of their implacable hostility is not any rubbishing of the temple, but is Jesus' continuous preaching.

PRAYER

Lord, we use often enough your saying, "My house will be a house
of prayer" of our own churches. Grant me there to listen to your voice in
words and in silence, in beauty and in wonder.

A CHALLENGE TO THE
AUTHORITY OF JESUS

THROUGHOUT THE GOSPEL, Jesus has been represented as a teacher. From the beginning the authority of his teaching has been shown also by his authority as a healer. Now it is as a teacher that his authority is challenged by the leaders of the temple. This is different from Mark's story, where the challenge was to his authority to purge or renew the temple. In Luke (in the previous scene) he has done little of this, but on the other hand, he has cleared the temple so that he may teach daily in it. So in Mark the challenge occurs simply when he comes back into the temple and is walking around—as though they took the first opportunity of meeting him again. In Luke, Jesus has been engaged on a stable ministry of preaching and proclaiming the good news in the temple, rivaling the temple teachers with his prophetic authority. It is to his teaching authority that the challenge is made.

A Rabbinic Controversy

THE CONTROVERSY TAKES a recognizable form. The first challenge is in fact a question: Who "ordained" Jesus? At the end of rabbinic training, when a rabbi reckons that he has taught his pupil all he knows, and the pupil is ready to teach, the rabbi confers authority by the imposition of hands on the pupil's head. No doubt some such transfer of authority existed already in Jesus' day. The continuity of the oral tradition of teaching the Law was already important: The oral tradition was held to stem from Moses himself, no less than the written text. It is, then, a question of the chain of authority.

A Feature of Jesus' Teaching

JESUS REPLIES TO the question with a counterquestion. Such a form of controversy is not unknown in the rabbinic texts, and indeed in other philosophical discussion, but it seems to have been a special feature of

Jesus' speech. Several of the Gospel controversies or discussions between Jesus and his opponents proceed in four steps:

(1) A question to Jesus from his opponents

(2) Jesus' counterquestion

(3) Unsatisfactory answer from the opponents

(4) Jesus silences his opponents

This form is used, for instance, in the discussion on divorce (not given in Luke) and on the tribute coin. It enables Jesus to challenge his opponents to think further and to question their assumptions. Often, also, Jesus' final answer widens their horizons and shocks them by going beyond what they had ever envisaged. Thus, on divorce Jesus refers them back, beyond the petty rules of how and when divorce is permitted, to the original purpose of the sexes, the union of two in one flesh. On the coin of tribute he is asked a question that is intended as a merely political booby trap. He couples to his straightforward answer the demand that they should also give to God "what belongs to God"—rather more than they had asked!

Two Details

THERE ARE TWO special points of interest in the story. The first is the demonstration of the respect in which John the Baptist was held. From the rest of Luke one would have little idea of this. His arrest is narrated before Jesus' baptism, so that he can seem to have been no more than a passing preacher to prepare the way. Mark and Matthew do indeed tell the story of his death, but only as a personal tale of intrigue, malice, and indulgence. It is only from the historian Josephus that we know the breadth of his influence, for Josephus says that Herod arrested him for fear of his rousing a revolt among the people. The respect in which he was held obviously outlived him.

Secondly, the story is instinct with a dreadful irony. In his lament over Jerusalem Jesus has bewailed that they did not recognize the moment of its visitation. Now we see this refusal in action. It is with obvious stubbornness that they refuse to acknowledge what they know in their heart of hearts to be the truth.

PRAYER

Grant me openness to the truth, however much it goes against my wishes and personal ideas. Spare me from the stubbornness that prevents me recognizing when I am wrong.

THE PARABLE OF THE WICKED TENANTS

LUKE FOLLOWS THE line of the parable he found in Mark with a few touches culled from Matthew and a few added of his own. In Mark this is one of two major story parables in his Gospel (the other being the sower), each of which is strategically placed at a turning point of the Gospel; this parable is placed to illustrate the whole of the relationship between Jesus and the Jerusalem authorities that is being played out in the final days of Jesus' ministry. Typical of Luke is the careful crescendo of maltreatment of the messengers: The first is thrashed and sent away empty-handed, the second thrashed, treated shamefully (being shamed is often a Lucan horror, as in the stories of the selfish householder, the unjust judge and the crafty steward) and sent away empty-handed, the third wounded and positively thrown out, all before the final crime.

The Vineyard of Israel

TO ANY WHO know the prophet Isaiah, the allusion is obviously to the lovely poem in Isaiah 5:

> *My beloved had a vineyard on a fertile hillside.*
> *He dug it, cleared it of stones, and planted it with red grapes.*
> *In the middle he built a tower, he hewed a press there too.*
> *He expected it to yield fine grapes: wild grapes were all it yielded.*
> *And now, citizens of Jerusalem and people of Judah,*
> *I ask you to judge between me and my vineyard . . .*
> *The vineyard of Yahweh Sabaoth is the House of Israel,*
> *and the people of Judah the plant he cherished.*

Perhaps Jesus' story was originally directed against the people of Judah as a whole rather than against its leaders, reflecting upon their refusal to accept his message, and so the failure of his proclamation of the kingdom.

It is possible that originally the rejection was the single point of the parable, with simply a crescendo of stubbornness as increasingly pressing messengers were sent. But, if Jesus understood himself as "the son," the allegory is obvious. It is made a little more obvious by Matthew and Luke: In Mark, naturally, the son is killed and his body thrown out of the vineyard. In Matthew and Luke he is thrown out first, before being killed. This accords more exactly with the death of Jesus, who was first taken outside the city before being executed. He follows in the line of the prophets who were rejected and maltreated.

But Luke, in particular, has no doubt that it applies directly to the leaders. He makes it explicit that the chief priests and scribes (rather than Mark's indeterminate "they") recognized that the parable was directed against themselves, and wanted to lay hands on him at that very moment. But they were deterred by the people (and again Luke uses the technical term that signifies the People of God). In Luke alone they had responded to the threat of the parable with "God forbid!"

The Lesson Reinforced

IN ALL THREE Synoptic Gospels the lesson of the parable is reinforced by a further quotation from Psalm 118 about the cornerstone. In a fine building, one for which the builders could afford to reject stones, this is a proud stone, properly speaking, the head of the corner. A solid and heavy stone, too, as Luke well knows when he illustrates the effects of collision with it, alluding to Isaiah 8:14, where the stone that crushes the opponents is the Lord God himself.

Matthew emphasizes constantly in his Gospel the failure and total rejection of Israel as a whole. He here adds that the kingdom will be taken away from them and given to another nation, which will bear fruit. It is important that Luke omits this comment: For him not all Israel is rejected, but some are saved and only the leaders persist in their rejection.

PRAYER
Lord, in your love you send to me messenger after messenger.
Let me respond to your love. There is also in the background the fear of
being crushed by stubborn refusal to recognize the cornerstone. Give me
a fear and reverence for your name.

ON PAYING TRIBUTE TO CAESAR

THERE FOLLOWS A pair of controversies between Jesus and his opponents, in which they are trying to catch him out on matters of politics and religion. Mark had put together a neat group of four such tussles, but Luke has already used one of them, the Great Commandment (10:25–28, no. 41), perhaps because there the lawyer who puts the question is praised rather than blamed, perhaps because Luke wants to attach to it the story of the good Samaritan.

The Trap Is Set

THE OBJECT OF these questioners is to trap Jesus, and they put to him a good question. It is a religious question as well as a political one, and it contains two different catches, concerning the tribute and the coin. The object was either to discredit or to incriminate this religious leader. They meant to fix him on the horns of a dilemma: Either he accepts paying taxes to Caesar and so makes himself liable to the accusation of disloyalty to Jewish nationalism, or he makes himself liable to the accusation of disloyalty to the Roman Empire. To pay the tribute implied recognition of the sovereignty of Caesar. When tribute was first imposed on a province of the Roman Empire, there were frequent revolts simply because people dislike paying taxes in general and to foreign powers in particular. Judea was no exception; the revolt of Judas the Galilean was still remembered, and is enshrined in the Gospel. But in Judea there was an additional cause of resentment and controversy. It was deep in the Jewish soul and theology that God alone is king. Therefore to recognize the sovereignty of another and earthly ruler is, at least on the surface, a betrayal of religious loyalty. At the dreadful climax of the trial of Jesus before Pilate in John's Gospel, when the leaders of the Jews declare, "We have no king but Caesar," they commit the ultimate act of betrayal and hypocrisy.

    The second catch concerns use of the coinage itself. The denarius carried an image of the emperor, so ran counter to the prohibition of graven images. The Jews could be very sensitive about this and made out that they were outraged when Pilate had some troops march through Judea carrying their eagle standards. The coin also had what could be regarded as an idolatrous inscription, describing the emperor as a god and the son of a god. Pilate again fell foul of this difficulty when he had golden inscriptions to the emperor put up on his residence in Jerusalem. Therefore the very use of the coinage could itself be regarded as an act of recognition of false gods. Luke lets the hypocrisy of the opponents of Jesus stand out all the more by making them immediately produce the coin, so to speak, out of their pockets. In Mark they do at least have to go and fetch one.

The Trap Is Sprung

JESUS' REACTION TO this trap may be considered on two completely different levels. On the level of the tricksters Jesus answers them in their own terms. He shows up their hypocrisy by making them produce the coin, which implies their own acceptance of Rome. It is attractive to picture that he uses this coin for his answer, pointing to the two prominent words inscribed on the coin itself: "Pay Caesar [pointing to the inscription CAES] what belongs to Caesar and God [pointing to the inscription DIV] what belongs to God." Already on this level Jesus evades their trap and turns the tables on his opponents. He gives them a straight answer, but balances any charge of disloyalty arising from the first half of the answer by adding the second half. His answers often go beyond what the original questioners hoped or foresaw, and here too he goes beyond by urging their loyalty to God, which in itself suggests some defect there.

On a more profound and important level, Jesus triumphs over his opponents by cutting through their petty concerns. To him the petty questions of tribal loyalty and political niceties are unimportant. His business is God's kingship. He is not concerned about graven images or the implications of recognition of the emperor, provided that the single essential is observed, to give to God what belongs to God.

REFLECTION

Pay Caesar what belongs to Caesar, and God what belongs to God.

THE RESURRECTION OF THE DEAD

THE QUESTION HERE comes from the Sadducees. They virtually ceased to exist in the Jewish War of A.D. 70, so that we know little about them except what Josephus tells us in his highly schematic presentation of the three parties of the Jews. They formed the priestly aristocracy, theoretically stemming from Zadok, the priest of King David. From their hereditary families were drawn the chief priests and even the high priest. In practice they were, under the Romans, the governing classes. They were traditionalists, rejecting recent developments in theology, such as belief in the resurrection, in spirits, and in angels. They seem to have been more interested in the smooth running of the country than in religious matters. Spirits and angels began to bulk large in popular imagination, theology, and literature from the return from Babylon onward, during the so-called Persian period and under Persian influence. Apart from "the angel of Yahweh," angels appear only in the later books of scripture. Belief in the resurrection of the dead dates from even later, being first attested at the time of the Maccabean Revolt in 167 B.C.

Life After Death

THE EVOLUTION OF belief in life after death is fascinating in itself. At the time of the patriarchs and until King David, the dead were thought of as "gathered to their fathers," as though sinking back into the identity of the ancestral tribe. The same idea still shows itself in the parable of Lazarus "in the bosom of Abraham." Later the idea of Sheol prevails, a place somehow under the earth, where the dead live a shadowy and powerless existence, like leaves in the dust, uncomfortable, restless, and deprived of God. When the Maccabean martyrs, however, gave their lives in defense of Judaism, belief in a general resurrection of the dead at the end of time comes to view: "The King of the world will raise us up, since we die for his laws, to live again forever" (2 Maccabees 7:9).

The Sadducees, not accepting this development of two centuries earlier, now attempt to test Jesus by ridiculing it. Their means of doing so is the theological conundrum produced by the levirate law: If one brother dies childless, his brother must marry his wife and raise up a child to continue the original brother's name and line (Deuteronomy 25:5).

Jesus' Reply

THE REPLY OF Jesus may again be considered on two levels, one immediate and one more profound. The first is that the Lord is the God of Abraham, the God of Isaac, and the God of Jacob. This is a way of using the contemporary literalist exegesis of the scriptures to show that God still *is* the God of these long-past personalities. They still exist, and God never deserts his own. Once he has taken them on, he will never leave them. This is a comforting and reassuring thought.

The other level is that they fundamentally misunderstand what is meant by the next world and the resurrection of the dead, if they think that it will be a mere reproduction of this present existence. Luke, who has several times shown a certain reserve toward matrimony, putting it as one of the possible obstacles to the kingdom, here underlines that one of the differences will concern marriage. There will be no marrying, since there will be no death and no need for physical reproduction. But on a more general basis, life will simply be different. To begin with, companionship and love will be different; there will be none of the exclusiveness necessary in marriage. Paul fills this out a little—but not much—in 1 Corinthians 15: "We shall all be changed." There will be continuity of personality, but bodies will no longer be physical in the same sense when they are taken up into the sphere of the divine. We must take it literally that "what no eye has seen and no ear has heard, what the human mind cannot visualize; all that God has prepared for those who love him" (1 Corinthians 2:9, quoting Isaiah 64:3).

PRAYER

Lord, God of Abraham, God of Isaac, and God of Jacob, there can be no fear of death, as you never desert us. I cannot envisage what this resurrection of the dead will be, but I know that I am safe in your hands.

CHRIST NOT ONLY SON
BUT LORD OF DAVID

THERE HAVE BEEN two questions from the representatives of the Jews. After the first, we are told that they could not catch him out and were silenced. The second group of questioners is even well enough disposed to praise Jesus, but again they did not dare ask him any more questions. After this Jesus himself takes the initiative to put them a question.

The title "Son of David" designates Jesus as the fulfillment of the Jewish tradition. The Jews in the first century lived in hope, and a central element of that hope was the fulfillment of the promises to David spoken by God through the prophet Nathan (2 Samuel 7). This we see already in the record of the annunciation, where they are echoed by the words of the angel. David was at once the figure of the ideal king and leader of his people and the figure of the darling of God. His massive sin (adultery with Bathsheba and cover-up murder of her husband, Uriah) followed by his wholehearted and prayerful repentance made him a sympathetic and attractive figure with whom any reflective person could identify. His later troubles made him an approachable model for all those who had their own troubles. His leadership of the people into a period of unprecedented prosperity made him also a symbol of gratitude and hope. Thus the designation of the Messiah as "Son of David" focuses many aspects of Israel's hope.

At first sight it is therefore surprising that Jesus questions this hope: How can the Messiah be Son of David? His puzzle needs some explanation. It is, of course, founded on the assumption, taken for granted at the time of Jesus but widely questioned today, that David is the author and singer of the psalms. It also plays on the expression "my Lord," and understands the two "Lords" differently: "The Lord (God) declared to my Lord (the Messiah) . . ." Jesus queries how David can call his descendant "my Lord." It should be that the descendant calls the ancestor "Lord," not the other way around. There must therefore be a descendant of

David, the Messiah, who is even greater than David himself. He is therefore not simply a descendant of David.

This psalm verse was treasured in the earliest Christian tradition also as an expression of the exaltation of Christ at the resurrection. The vindication of Jesus on the third day was described in several different ways. The empty tomb was only one of these, the appearances of the risen Lord experienced by his disciples another. The inner reality and significance of these had to be described in terms of images, of which "taking his seat at the right hand" of the Father was a central one. Other images are the exaltation and glorification of Jesus, expressing his sharing in God's glory.

Jesus himself seems to have been slightly hesitant about this title. Perhaps he was cautious about the possible political overtones of kingship. It was, in fact, a title used also by rebel leaders of the time in the hope of gathering support by appeal to the tradition of David. When Peter, at Luke 9:20, hails Jesus as "the Christ of God," Jesus does not joyfully welcome this recognition. Instead, he chides them, and tells them not to tell anyone; is this acceptance or not? When Bartimaeus twice hails him as Son of David (18:38, 39), Jesus neither rebukes nor encourages him. Only at the trial before the high priest does he accept the title of Christ, that is, Messiah, and even then he quickly reinterprets it.

The Gospels of Matthew and Luke, however, show the full importance of this title. In Matthew, Jesus is several times hailed as "Son of David," and the whole of Matthew 1 is devoted to showing how Jesus came to be incorporated, by divine intervention, into the House of David through Joseph's adoption. Similarly, in Luke's story of the annunciation to Mary, the angel tells her that "the Lord God will give him the throne of his ancestor David" (1:32). That Jesus was seen as the Messiah is clear also from the title early given—probably with a slight tone of mockery—to his followers at Antioch, "Christians," or "followers of the Christ/Messiah."

PRAYER
You are the Christ, the son of the living God. Let me treasure
this name of "Christian," which was given to your followers so early. If
it has this tone of mockery, let me feel it an honor to share in your
mockery and to follow you with a devotion beyond all reason
and all limit.

THE SCRIBES AND THE POOR WIDOW

THE CONFRONTATION THAT has been going on between Jesus and the Jerusalem leaders ends with a contrast between the scribes and a widow. In this, Luke follows Mark, who has the same contrast between the two groups. At this point in the Gospel, Matthew gives a full-scale attack on scribes and Pharisees together (Matthew 23). In his earlier diatribe against the Pharisees and the scribes, Luke had made a distinction between the two groups, giving some charges against the Pharisees and some against the scribes. Now he carries on this careful distinction by making his attack on the scribes alone, taking over virtually unchanged the criticisms given in Mark. He has already made sparing use of the Matthean material in Luke 11. The chief criticism here is the self-importance betrayed by their craving for front seats at meals in the synagogue. Luke has already given us an example of the arrogance of the Pharisees in the parable of the Pharisee and the tax collector, and of the importance of prominent positions at table in his warning at 14:8–11. The exact point here is perhaps the self-importance of the lawyers, a danger for teachers at any level!

The final criticism is hypocritical avarice, in which there is a neat contrast with the following section: The scribes swallow up the property of widows, while the poor widow puts all her livelihood into the treasury. In the ancient world widows were the very paradigm of helplessness. In theory, in Hebrew society they reverted to the care of their fathers-in-law, but in practice they were often left destitute. In the New Testament there are several mentions of the special care to be taken of them. So to swallow up the property of such people is obviously an extreme case of callous greed, and the widow's gift is obviously an extreme case of generosity. Her two coins are called *lepta*, which literally means "light" or "fine," mere wafers of bronze. The "treasury" was not money for the temple; it appears from the rabbinic literature to have contained a fund for distribution to the poor. It is all the more touching that the widow, herself already destitute, should give money for distribution for other poor people. It is often the poor who are most thoughtful and generous to other people in need.

It was a pious practice in the first century for elderly people to come to Jerusalem and take up residence there for their last years to prepare for death. Perhaps the most famous case at that time was the rich Persian queen, Helen of Adiabene, whose ample tomb is still visible in Jerusalem. Not all were so well off. That widows and their needs were an issue in the earliest Christian community in Jerusalem is made clear from the dispute in Acts 6, which led to the appointment of the Seven. The widows of the "Hellenists" in the Christian community were being overlooked in the distribution of alms in favor of those of the "Hebrews." It is not clear exactly who these two parties represent. They possibly refer to two different language groups, possibly two different cultural divisions. At any rate, their number and the neglect of them was important enough to require significant community arrangements for them. Luke will have had this in mind when he juxtaposed the two contrasting cases, applying the teaching about God's care for the poor and the danger of wealth that have been so prominent throughout the Gospel.

PRAYER

Lord, save me from hypocrisy, and especially from making excuses to cover up my own laziness or lack of generosity.

AN APOCALYPSE (I)
THE DESTRUCTION OF JERUSALEM

ALL THE SYNOPTIC Gospels at this stage, just before the final events of Jesus' ministry in Jerusalem, have a long section in which Jesus foretells to his disciples the future trials, and, in highly symbolic language, sketches out the whole future of his community. Mark's version was somewhat differently oriented from Luke's.

Warning Signs

IN MARK, JESUS' prediction of the future is given on the Mount of Olives, looking across the Kedron Valley to Jerusalem. It is still a breathtaking view to see across the valley the shimmering white houses of Jerusalem and the gigantic esplanade or platform which is all that is left of the temple. In Luke, the prediction takes place within the temple itself. Jesus takes the temple as his own platform for proclamation. So this prediction is centered on the temple itself rather than simply on the city of Jerusalem. The "offerings" to which Jesus refers are gone now, but some of the "fine stonework" remains in the lower courses of the wall. Herodian monumental masonry is unmistakable: huge, perfectly smoothed blocks with delicately beveled edges to give a play of light on the honey-colored stone.

The chief importance of the first four verses of the discourse is to defuse panic. The drift of Luke's thought is best seen by two deliberate changes he makes from Mark. Mark is concerned about the end of all things; Luke concentrates his attention on the end of Jerusalem. So where Mark has the cosmically threatening "Tell us when all these things are to be *brought to a conclusion*" (Mark 13:4, a literal translation) and uses the ominous prophetic image of *birth pangs* (13:8), Luke tones these down respectively to "What sign will there be that it is *about to take place*" and the vaguer "There will be *terrifying events and great signs* from heaven." The messianic movements alluded to in verse 8 were particularly frequent after A.D. 44 in Judea, and the buildup to the disastrous Jewish revolt of A.D. 66 must have been clear for all to see.

The Persecution of the Disciples

IT WAS IMPORTANT that the early church, struggling under persecution even before the siege of Jerusalem (v. 12), should understand that Jesus had foreseen and foretold it all, that none of it was without the will and protection of the Master. In the Acts of the Apostles we may see all these predictions being literally fulfilled, as the disciples are arraigned before synagogues and imprisoned, as Paul is brought before governors (Felix and Festus) and kings (Herod Agrippa and Berenice).

Mark had already contained these predictions. But in Luke there is a sharper focus: *"I myself* shall give you an eloquence and a wisdom. . . ."* In Mark the sentence was in the theological passive: "Say whatever is given to you. . . ." But here Jesus makes it clear that he himself will be inspiring and guiding them. So in Acts, the Spirit of Jesus is constantly with them as they carry on by their miracles and witness and sufferings the life of Jesus himself in the world. The perseverance to the death which will paradoxically win them their lives (v. 19) has been a keynote of Luke's Gospel.

The Siege of Jerusalem

MARK HAD FORETOLD the "appalling abomination" (Mark 13:14), which is most probably understood as the statue the emperor Gaius nearly succeeded in setting up in the temple (he died before arrangements were complete). This was interpreted as one of the signs of the end time, the cataclysm of the last days, so dreadful that "if the Lord had not shortened that time, *no human being* would have survived" (Mark 13:20). Luke's focus is again limited to the siege of Jerusalem. He includes the name of the city twice (vv. 20, 24), and speaks clearly of slaughter in battle and dispersal of *prisoners of war* to all nations. In fact, the Jewish population of Rome was hugely swelled by the prisoners brought there after the capture of Jerusalem to build (among other things) the still-impressive Arch of Titus. For Luke, the sack of Jerusalem was theologically important, the fulfillment of Jesus' prophecies of the fate of the city that would not recognize the time of its visitation.

PRAYER
If only you had recognized the way to peace!

AN APOCALYPSE (II)
THE COMING OF THE SON OF MAN

ONCE THE FATE of Jerusalem has been foretold, the tone changes and the horizon broadens. The transition from the end of Jerusalem to the wider perspective is smoothly operated: "And Jerusalem will be trampled down by the Gentiles until *their* time is complete." He goes on to speak no longer of Jerusalem, but of "nations" and "the world." Luke gives the same awe-inspiring picture of cosmic cataclysm as does Mark, in terms of imagery drawn from the prophets of the Old Testament about the Day of the Lord, a bewildering chaos of sun, moon, and stars. His picture is completed and intensified (v. 26) by the terrified reaction of human beings, utterly bewildered and fainting away at the very expectation of what is about to occur.

But, by contrast, for Christ's disciples, Jesus' audience, it will be a time of hope: As soon as these signs begin, they should lift up their heads, for their liberation is near. The signs are the encouraging presage of the approach of the kingship of God. The signs are expressed in terms of prophetic and Old Testament imagery, but we are told that they are as clear as the leaves budding in spring.

The Timing of Events

THE IMMEDIATE PUZZLE comes later, with regard to the timing: What can be meant by "before this generation has passed away, all will have taken place"? Was Jesus wrong? Luke wrote these words some half-century after the time of Jesus' ministry, when the generation addressed by Jesus had surely passed away. It is hard to believe that he (and also Mark and Matthew) would have included them if they had already been proved wrong. Some clue of Luke's view may be gleaned from 9:27: In his version of Mark 9:1 he leaves out the last three words, "There are some standing here who will not taste death till they see the kingdom of God *come with power.*" So we may deduce that they will see the kingdom of God, but not with power. Similarly, in Luke's version of the trial scene at 22:69, Jesus stresses the immediacy, *"From now on,* the Son of Man will be seated at the right hand of the Power." It must be, therefore, that Luke sees the Passion and resurrection as somehow the accomplishment of the kingship of God. This is why the theme of Jesus' own kingship is so strongly stated at the time of the Passion and resurrection (see no. 68 in this book). The accomplishment of God's kingship is not to be understood as something that happens in a single moment; it comes in stages, with several decisive moments before the final crisis.

The Cares of Life

LUKE'S CONCERN IS seen strongly from the conclusion to his discourse. He has frequently shown his wary concern for the distractions of wealth and business interests. Now (v. 34) he emphasizes particularly the pleasures of food and drink as a distraction, as exemplified in the drunkenness of the steward in 12:45. Distraction is very operative, for the stress is on the suddenness and unexpectedness of the arrival of the Day. Once again Luke stresses his message of perseverance in prayer. Now that the expectation of a speedy coming of the triumphant Christ has cooled, it is all the more important to encourage perseverance in their vocation. But Luke uses traditional language and images, which already occur in 1 Thessalonians 5:2–3. One fascinating little verbal detail is the image of the trap being sprung. The same letters in Aramaic can be translated either "birth pangs" or "trap." So 1 Thessalonians speaks of birth pangs and Luke of a trap, both perhaps representing a different translation of the original Aramaic words of Jesus.

PRAYER

Keep me alert to the coming of your kingdom, at cock-crow, noon, or evening. I do not expect it to come for me in one swoop. You offer it to me again and again in the circumstances of life. Let me embrace it each time, till I finally see the kingship of God come in glory.

JUDAS BETRAYS JESUS

THIS PASSAGE BEGINS the Passion narrative, the climax of the Gospel. The Gospels have been described as "Passion narratives with extended introduction," and here everything comes to fulfillment. The earliest tradition of Christian proclamation was, as we see in Paul, centered on Jesus' death and resurrection, and it has been suggested that Mark's Passion narrative is the earliest piece of continuous writing in the Gospels, taken over by Mark from an earlier source. This opinion now seems less likely, and it is more probable that Mark himself put together the sections of the narrative. In some ways Luke is closer to Mark in the Passion narrative than anywhere else. On the other hand, this Gospel does have clear distinctions from Mark, which will add up to quite a different pattern. The Gospel of John similarly has its own reading of the Passion story, and there are some distinct similarities between Luke and John as opposed to Mark and Matthew. But again, the Gospel writers were not mere chroniclers, but show by their narratives the lessons for Christians which they see in the events of Jesus' suffering and death.

The Betrayal

ALL KINDS OF motives have been suggested for Judas' action, the most widespread being that he was a thief and cared only for money (as suggested by John 12:6). His nationalist name, the same as that of the great leader Judas the Maccabee, has prompted the suggestion that he had hoped Jesus would be a nationalist military leader, and that he "shopped" him on finally discovering that he had no such intentions. Recently it has even been suggested that far from betraying Jesus, he really "handed him over" in good faith to further Jesus' own plans. Luke and John 13:27 are not interested in Judas' psychology, and attribute the action to Satan, who enters into Judas. This is the moment to which Luke had looked forward when, at the end of the temptation story, he had said that the devil left Jesus until the opportune moment.

The Failure of Jesus

IT HAS BEEN asked how Jesus could have made the mistake of choosing as one of the twelve foundation stones of the new Israel a disciple who would betray him. Not that he was very successful in choosing stalwart, reliable, quick learners who understood his message and persevered in their support for him! Nor, for that matter, did he succeed in founding the renewed kingship of God, which he came to proclaim. Part of the tragedy of his death is that when he hung on the cross, his mission was in tatters; when he died, his mission should have died with him. Part of the vindication of his unquestioning obedience to his Father was that against all human likelihood the Twelve (or the Eleven) were strengthened by his Spirit to establish the new Israel.

Luke's insistence that Jesus taught daily in the temple makes a betrayal slightly strange: If they wanted to arrest Jesus, they had had plenty of opportunity to do so. On the other hand, if, as Luke insists twice, they wanted to do it "apart from the crowd," they would presumably wish to avoid an arrest in the temple, where a guide would be needed to find Jesus among the hordes of pilgrims assembled for Passover. Josephus (who constantly exaggerates numbers) gives a normal figure of over one million pilgrims.

The Arresting Party

THE PHARISEES DISAPPEAR entirely from the scene during the Passion in both Mark and Luke. They were not prepared to take their opposition to the stage of blood. The arrest will be on the initiative of the temple authorities. According to Luke, Judas' pact was made with the chief priests and the *strategoi*, normally a military office. John 18:3 mentions a *speira* at the arrest; this would normally be a detachment of Roman auxiliaries, but it could also be native troops of the province. There is nothing to show definitely that the Romans were involved in the process from the beginning, and throughout the Passion story Luke at least is eager to play down Roman involvement.

PRAYER

The deeper the companionship, Lord, the easier it is for me to betray you
By your friendship you lay yourself open. Grant that I may respond to
this trust.

PREPARATIONS FOR THE PASSOVER SUPPER

The Passover Festival

THE PASSOVER FESTIVAL now begins to have major importance in the Gospel, being mentioned repeatedly, in almost every verse of this section. The word "Passover" does not have an equivalent meaning to the Hebrew word *pesach;* it was coined by that most brilliant and original of English translators, William Tyndale, first appearing in 1530. It was not, as it is in Christianity, the greatest festival of all in the year, but was one of the three great feasts that all faithful Jews would, if possible, celebrate at Jerusalem. It commemorated the liberation of the Hebrews from slavery in Egypt and the covenant by which they became God's people in the desert. It was therefore the foundation festival of the people.

From the ritual of the meal, one can see that it was built on an older festival of pastoral nomads. It was possibly connected with moon worship, since it was celebrated at the full moon, the first full moon after the spring equinox (now March 21). It has all the features of a meal of nomads: unleavened bread, roast rather than boiled meat (to save on water and cooking pots), herbs rather than the vegetables of a sedentary people. At the beginning of spring each year a tribe of nomadic pastors would move from their winter to their summer pastures. This was the meal before their departure, when they sacrificed a prime animal from the flocks to win the favor of the gods and turn away evil spirits. This sacred meal was "baptized" to commemorate the greatest trek of all, the Exodus, when the Egyptians were eventually forced into letting their Hebrew slaves go.

Later, when Israel became sedentary and planted crops, this pastoral feast was combined with the agricultural feast of the first cutting of corn. The keynote of this was the purity of a fresh beginning, expressed in the jettisoning of all last year's leaven, and the eating of unleavened bread for a whole week. Both these elements contribute to the Christian meaning of the festival.

The Date of the Last Supper

THE CHRISTIAN EUCHARIST, the commemoration of the last supper, has the character of a paschal meal. The Synoptic Gospels all speak of the preparation for a paschal supper, and Jesus speaks explicitly of "the room for me to eat the Passover." But the Gospel of John, which makes particular use of the symbolism of Jesus as the paschal lamb, places his death on the day *before* Passover, at the hour when the paschal lambs were slaughtered. There are, then, three possibilities: Either one of the two chronologies is incorrect, or Jesus celebrated the paschal meal by a different calendar (such as that used in Qumran), or the last supper was not a paschal meal. In this case it could be classified as a fellowship meal with a paschal character.

The Preparations

JESUS' SENDING OF two disciples is very similar to the mission to fetch a mount for his entry into Jerusalem. There is the same air of mystery and of authority. We are not told of any preparatory arrangements. The man with the water pot would be easily recognized; it was almost unthinkable that a man should carry a water pot. I have never seen such a thing in my visits to the region. It was, and still is, women's work! He simply seems to know and to respond to the instructions. Jesus is seen as the authoritative prophet, who knows beforehand what will happen, and whose instructions are obeyed to the letter. This prescience is part of Jesus' foreknowledge of the whole course of events of the Passion. With the great influx of pilgrims into Jerusalem for the festival, there was no doubt a thriving business in renting out rooms for groups of nonresidents, but on this occasion the process does not give the impression of a commercial transaction.

Luke gives more detail than the other Gospels about the envoys, naming them Peter and John. In the Acts these work together as a pair of envoys sent down together to Samaria to confirm their reception into the Christian community.

PRAYER

Lord, your paschal meal is so solemn and so sacred that even the preparations have their solemnity. Grant me to prepare myself with due seriousness for your eucharistic banquet.

THE INSTITUTION OF THE EUCHARIST

THREE PRELIMINARY REMARKS must be made. This section makes no attempt to describe the paschal meal with all its ritual. In fact, we know little about the ritual of the meal at this time, and can reconstruct it only from much later texts. But the Gospel account is concerned only with the eucharist, not with the meal on which it was probably built. The story is a liturgical text, an account to justify the eucharistic practice of the author's own day by Jesus' action. This is shown by the words "Do this in remembrance of me," which legitimate and indeed command the continuance of the rite. It is classic for a liturgical text to include the justification for the performance of the rite. Secondly, there is a fascinating trace of the earliest tradition of church life. The account of the institution is given also by Paul (1 Corinthians 11:23–26) as part of the tradition he learned by heart and passed on to his converts. Careful observation reveals a pattern of small differences between the accounts given by Mark/Matthew and by Luke/Paul. The former has more trace of Semitic culture, the latter of Greek. So it may be that the former tradition was handed down through the Semitic churches, the latter through the Greek-speaking churches. Thirdly, some manuscripts of this section give a shorter text than others, verses 19b–20 being absent from the Western tradition; we shall opt for the view that the whole section comes from Luke.

The Scene

LUKE IS CLEARLY using his predecessors, Mark and probably Matthew, but he makes a deliberate change in the order of events. Why? Firstly, he removes all mention of Judas' treachery from this scene, and replaces it with Jesus' declaration of his ardent yearning to eat this paschal meal with his disciples; he wants to concentrate on the climactic nature of this moment, and to avoid distracting from its peace by the disharmony of betrayal. Secondly, he puts before the account of the institution a double emphatic declaration that Jesus will not eat the pasch or drink the cup again until the kingdom of God comes. Then immediately Jesus proceeds to give them the bread and the cup; is he suggesting that in some way the kingdom comes at that moment? True, he is not said himself to eat and drink, but the emphasis on the coming of the kingdom is in any case massive.

The Covenant

THE COVENANT ON Sinai by which God formed a people for himself was sealed by the blood of sacrifice sprinkled over the people. Thereafter in Judaism, each newborn male child was bound into the covenant by circumcision, that is, by "the blood of the covenant." Now Jesus declares a new covenant in his own blood. This is the moment of the formation of a new people of God, parallel to God's covenant with Israel in the desert. It is sealed by the blood of Jesus. So Jesus' action and words are prophetic, both giving meaning to and deriving their meaning from the events of the Passion that are to come.

To drink blood was a strong taboo in Judaism. All blood had to be drained from meat before eating. They held that the life of a creature was in the blood, and so it was sacred to, dedicated to, owned by God. Therefore when Jesus, despite this taboo, offers them his blood, he is offering them a share in his life.

"Poured Out for You"

THE FINAL WORDS of Jesus allude to the Song of the Suffering Servant in Isaiah 53. This poem speaks of a servant of the Lord who gives his life for the sins of others, and, after humiliation and death, is vindicated by God himself. They are a precious sign of his own whole view of the Passion, giving focus to many other sayings, such as "the Son of Man has come not to be served but to serve." If this is Jesus' own interpretation of the events, it comes as a climax of his ministry of service. From such a precious touch it is possible to see the orientation and expectation that lies behind so many other events and sayings.

PRAYER

Lord, you longed to eat the Passover with your disciples. Keep alive in me the longing to join you in the meal that bespeaks your sacrifice.

PARTING INSTRUCTIONS (I)

THE PARTING SPEECH by a leader or great figure was a convention both in Greek and in Jewish literature. The most famous example in Greek literature is probably that of Socrates before his voluntary death. In Hebrew, famous examples are the final speeches of Moses in the book of Deuteronomy, and, outside the Bible, the *Testaments of the Twelve Patriarchs,* written in the first century, though attributed to the twelve sons of Jacob. Obviously the final hours are a time when the great man's sayings are listened to with most attention, and also a time when the great man naturally makes dispositions for the future. It is not uncommon for this convention to be combined with the convention Luke has already used several times, that of giving important teaching at a dinner (e.g., on forgiveness, at the supper given by Simon the Pharisee).

The Betrayer

MARK AND MATTHEW present before the institution of the eucharist a dramatic little scene that points out Judas as the traitor. Luke defers this till afterward, perhaps to avoid darkening that event, and reduces it to one saying of Jesus. The emphasis is on the disgrace of the betrayal, not on the personal identity of the betrayer, for to break a shared table fellowship by such a betrayal was sickeningly odious. At the same time, Jesus underlines his foreknowledge and the predestined inevitability of his Passion. He is still being represented as the prophet who knows the future and the secrets of human hearts.

The Grandeur of Service

THE CENTRAL TEACHING Jesus gives in this farewell address after the supper concentrates on the role of the leaders in the community. Luke has saved up these two pieces of teaching about discipleship, which occur earlier in the other Gospels, in order to give them additional emphasis by their placement at this solemn moment. They are linked by the theme of the kingdom, and teach about the responsibility of playing a leading role in the kingdom. They are given added emphasis by their position. This is the only general teaching in the address. It is flanked by pieces on two contrasting individuals, Judas, who was faithful and later fell away, Peter, who fell away and later returned to strengthen his brethren.

The first subsection is on dominance and ministering. Luke's teaching is all the more impressive because it is gentle. He moderates Mark's harsh presentation, "those who seem to rule over the nations *dominate* them," for Mark's word means almost "grind them down, domineer over them." Instead, he introduces a sort of courtly and formal grandeur, with his "lord," "king," "benefactor" (an honorific title often used in the royal courts of the east). Again Luke's cultured and leisured background is visible; we have frequently seen it in his easy use of financial terms, and in his warning against the dangers of wealth.

For "have authority" Luke uses the word that derives from "make possible," allowing the conception that the real purpose of authority is to open up possibilities, to be a "facilitator." Another word frequently used for "rule" is *arche*, which also means "beginning"; an authority is one who makes beginnings. Nevertheless, this is not the whole of the Christian concept, which is to be a servant. Here Luke introduces, aptly for the context of a supper, the contrast between those relaxing at table and those serving. One is reminded of the principal scene at the Johannine last supper, when Jesus washes the feet of the disciples—to the horror of Peter. The same word for "serve" will be used by Luke of those who distribute food to the poor in Acts 6. It is significant that the word "slave" is not used. There is nothing demeaning or shaming about this service; it is simply a matter of attending to the needs of others before one's own comfort. The emphasis on this nature of Christian service almost suggests a knowledge of future centuries of the Christian Church, when, despite such titles as "minister," a certain grandeur has seemed unavoidably associated with authority in the Church.

PRAYER

Lord, grant me to understand and put into practice the truth that all ministry in your church is centered on the needs of those to whom we minister. Help me to put myself into their position and see how I can gently guide them to you.

PARTING INSTRUCTIONS (II)

THE SECOND SECTION of general teaching on the disciples remains with the image of kingship. It focuses on the kingship of Jesus, which has been becoming so prominent in the narrative since the story of Bartimaeus. It combines this with the image of the dinner table, with its promise of feasting in the kingdom.

But Jesus also promises the disciples that they will sit on thrones as judges in the kingdom. Here the image is of a court, for in the ancient world people did not sit on chairs at the table, but reclined on couches or mats. This same promise occurs in Matthew. Then it will take place at "the rebirth." Here there is no mention of that, and one is left wondering when it is to occur. Is Luke envisaging the second coming or an event that is closer? The account of the institution of the eucharist has already suggested that the kingdom is now in some way being accomplished at the Passion. One possible interpretation of the parable of the pounds (see no. 68) is that Jesus is to return as king in the narrative of the Acts, and the moment when he bestows authority on his faithful disciples has occurred already then. In this case Jesus is promising them that they will exercise authority over the new Israel, which is even then being created by the new covenant in his blood, namely the community Luke will chronicle in the Acts.

Peter

IN EACH OF the Gospels a special place is given to Peter. In the Synoptic Gospels he is the only one of the disciples who has much more than a walk-on part. Peter is constantly the spokesman of the group. At the same time, he is the most prominent failure, and his denial of Jesus at the trial is deeply etched into every Christian mind. Nevertheless, his part in the future of the community is emphasized in each Gospel. They may or may not all go back to the same basic saying, but each Gospel contains some passage on Peter's position.

He is the first of the disciples to be called by the lakeside. In Mark's story of the empty tomb, forgiveness of Peter and his reconciliation are specially noted by, "You must go and tell his disciples *and Peter* . . ." In Matthew there is no such reconciliation; the last we see or hear of Peter is his bursting into tears when the cock crows. But his position in the community is assured by the promises of Jesus made at Caesarea Philippi: "You are Peter and on this rock I will build my community." John's statement comes in his final chapter at the lakeside, with the triple commission (corresponding to the triple denial) to "Feed my sheep."

In Luke, Peter has frequently been given special attention, such as a slight emphasis by having a named part (for example, in arranging the room for the paschal meal). Now Jesus in his prophetic role foretells Peter's denial, but only *after* he has foretold his conversion. The heart of the pronouncement is the promise that Peter will strengthen his brothers. This is perhaps a more active and continuous role even than that of being the foundation rock as in Matthew. In his final disposition Luke's Jesus makes sure of stressing the organized structure of the community he leaves to carry on his work.

The Final Testing

THE LAST SECTION of the farewell speech prepares for the sequel. It predicts the full horror of the testing by announcing that the normal conditions of preaching the kingdom are suspended. These were imposed on the missioners in Luke 10, and were perfectly satisfactory then. But now is a time of violence and unprecedented stress.

At the same time, reassurance is given by the quotation from scripture: It was all foreseen and willed by God in the expression of his covenant. The little quotation from Isaiah 53, "He was counted as one of the rebellious," is enough to recall the whole poem, so frequently occurring during the Passion narrative. Allusions to it are contained in the frequent mention of the silence of Jesus ("like a sheep dumb before its shearers"), the mockery, the tomb with the rich. The detailed comparison, however, is only a vehicle for the interpretation of the event as a whole: At his Passion Jesus takes on the sins of all and himself atones for them. This is the meaning contained in each of the detailed allusions.

REFLECTION

By the time the cock crows today, you will have denied three times that you know me.

169

THE MOUNT OF OLIVES

THE SCENE OF the agony in the garden as related by Mark has undergone a radical restructuring in Luke. In Mark there were two centers of emphasis, the failure of the disciples and the horror of Jesus. The failure of the disciples is stressed by a typically Marcan triple repetition: Jesus comes back to the disciples three times to find them sleeping. This is more important to Mark even than the triple prayer of Jesus, for the second prayer is barely mentioned and the third not at all. However, Jesus' horror and fear at his approaching arrest and torture are fully expressed. The words used for his "terror and anguish" are very strong, denoting almost that he was stunned and beside himself with fear. The word used for his falling to the ground suggests that he was stumbling and falling repeatedly, almost uncontrollably.

Luke's Recasting of the Scene

THE LUCAN EMPHASIS is quite different. Here the triple scene is welded into one. The prayer of Jesus is presented as an example for the disciples to follow, for the whole episode is bracketed by "Pray, so that you may not be put to the test" at beginning and end. The disciples themselves are to pray, not merely to wait while Jesus goes and prays. The persecution of Jesus in the Passion is an example the disciples also will undergo, and in the same way his prayer beforehand is a model for them to imitate. There is no mention here of the failure of the disciples, or indeed of their presence at all, though we were told at the beginning that they followed him, and so shared with him in this prayerful scene. When they are finally mentioned—when the prayer of Jesus is finished—there is no blame attached to them. They are "sleeping for sheer grief": This suggests merely that they were so sad, they could no longer stand up.

    The Jesus presented is entirely in control, and the emphasis is on his calm and submissive prayer. There is no stumbling or falling to the ground, no bewilderment in the prayer. Instead, Jesus kneels calmly down, as Christians will in fervent prayer. He then expresses his prayer only conditionally, "If it is your will . . ." (There again he is a model for disciples, for Paul prays the same phrase before his arrest in Acts 21:14.) At the end of his prayer Jesus stands upright with full dignity.

What, then, of the agony and the sweat? (Verses 43–44 are in fact omitted by some good manuscripts of the Gospel.) It is often carelessly said that Jesus sweated drops of blood, and the saying has even become proverbial. But Luke says only that his sweat was *"like* drops of blood falling to the ground." The comparison may be of size or of flow. A most plausible interpretation that brings all these elements together is based on the word *agon,* which normally means an athletic contest. Jesus is sweating in anticipation of his struggle, as an athlete whose adrenaline is flowing before the start of a race or competition. This reading of the text agrees well with the appearance of a strengthening angel. There is a strikingly similar scene in Daniel 10:15–19: Before his great task of prophecy Daniel prostrates himself on the ground through lack of strength, and is comforted and strengthened by an angel.

The Christian Tradition

JESUS' PRAYER BEFORE his Passion is reflected in a quite different scene in John 12:27. Here there is virtually only the words of his prayer and an allusion to an angel, no mention of the Mount of Olives, no scene of falling to his knees, no sharing with the disciples. The Johannine Jesus, for whom the cross and resurrection are the moment of glory and exaltation, does not pray to be spared the hour, but embraces it willingly. Similarly, Hebrews 5:7 relates, "He offered prayers and entreaty, with loud cries and with tears, to the one who had power to save him from death, and so learned obedience." The tradition of the prayer of Jesus before his Passion was, therefore, preserved in various forms in different traditions of the early community. Each evangelist presented this as part of his own presentation of the Passion.

PRAYER

You sometimes put me, Lord, before trials that seem beyond my strength. Give me confidence in your power and love to guide me through these trials and to share your Passion with you.

171

THE ARREST

THE NUMBER OF pilgrims in Jerusalem for the Passover was immense. The polyglot list of peoples who heard the apostles at Pentecost, however, gives the same impression. To celebrate the feast properly, pilgrims were supposed to spend the night in Jerusalem, but the numbers were such that the theoretical limits of the city were extended to include the Mount of Olives. It would be no easy task to find Jesus and his small group among all the throngs on the hillside. Mark and Matthew tell us that the place was called Gethsemane, but that means only "Garden of Oil/Olives," which on a hill covered with olive orchards would not be very specific. Hence the need for Judas to lead the arresting party to the place where Jesus would be.

Jesus continues to be in control of the scene. In Mark and Matthew, after the turmoil of the prayer scene, Jesus regains control of himself and the situation. In Luke's account he never lost it. But it is additionally stressed by two factors. The first is a contrast: The disciples resort to violence, with an excited cry that could be rendered, "What about our hitting out with a sword?" The question to Jesus and Jesus' silence makes its impression. Jesus by contrast even now continues his mission of healing, as indeed he will continue it right up to the end by his forgiveness of the good thief. Secondly, Jesus continues his mission of forgiveness. While Judas is still approaching, Jesus offers him a last chance, asking him whether he really intends what he is about to do, and again, with the juxtaposition of "betray" and "kiss," stressing the treachery of the deed. Jesus' gentle offer contrasts vividly with Judas' hard refusal. There is surely a contrast here also with the next occasion when Jesus offers repentance: After Peter's denial "the Lord turned and looked straight at Peter, and Peter remembered the Lord's words . . ." Peter repents, but Judas does not.

The Hour of Darkness

JESUS INTIMATES THAT the situation is, in one way, beyond human control. There is no hint that human responsibility is suspended, but there are more than human forces at work: "This is your hour; this is the reign of darkness." There is a suggestion of the same supernatural forces as at 22:3, when "Satan entered into Judas." There are two curious links here with the Gospel of John. Throughout that Gospel, Jesus has been looking forward to his "hour." John treats the whole event of the Passion and resurrection as one single moment, the single hour of his Passion and resurrection, which is the moment of his exaltation not only onto the cross, but to his Father, the moment also of his glorification. In Luke the same concept of "hour" is used, but now it is the hour of his enemies. More similar to the Gospel of John is the use of the image of darkness: "As soon as Judas had taken the piece of bread he went out. It was night," says John 13:30. This rejoins the imagery of the sons of light and the sons of darkness that is so common in the contemporary texts from Qumran. Indeed, Luke has also used this symbol, for instance in the *Benedictus*, "to give light to those who live in darkness and the shadow dark as death."

The Faithful Disciples

ONE MOST IMPORTANT difference between Luke's presentation of the scene and that of the other Synoptic Gospels is that there is no mention of desertion by the disciples. For Mark this is the moment of desertion. The icon of desertion in Mark is, of course, the young man who in order to flee leaves behind the sheet that is his sole covering. The disciples left all to follow Jesus; now he (ludicrously and with some wit) leaves all to escape from Jesus' company. In Luke we have been constantly reminded that the disciples are those who have stayed with Jesus in his trials. This is exemplified in the Passion. There is no word of their flight now, and at the cross "all his friends," as well as the women, are present (23:49) and faithful to the end.

PRAYER

Lord, we all sometimes feel betrayed by those we trust. Grant that I may face them with your gentleness, your spirit of forgiveness, and your outgoing offer of friendship.

PETER'S DENIALS AND THE MOCKERY OF JESUS

The Historical Difficulty

THERE MUST HAVE been in the tradition various components of the story of Jesus' examination by the Jewish authorities, which the evangelists felt free to dispose and arrange somewhat differently. The Gospel of John gives a decision by the council to get rid of Jesus long before, immediately after the raising of Lazarus; when Jesus has been taken into custody there is only an interrogation by Annas, the high priest's father-in-law (though Jesus is so much master of that scene that it should almost be called an interrogation *of* Annas) without any further Jewish trial. Mark and Matthew give a sort of trial, leading up to a verdict of guilt, by the high priest Caiaphas, sandwiched between the elements of Peter's denial of his master. This is a typical "Marcan sandwich," the triple denial of Peter contrasting with Jesus' triple stand against his accusers. The trial is immediately followed by mockery and abuse of Jesus by some unnamed people, presumably members of the council.

What actually happened in that night it is impossible to tell. We cannot reestablish how closely related the tradition was to eyewitness testimony. We do not even know the code of law under which a trial would have occurred. The legal regulations we do have form a purely theoretical body of law, which was formulated by the successors of the Pharisees at least a century later, and was never even envisaged as the law code of any real national judicature. The chief priests and Sadducees who ruled Judea in the time of Jesus had long ceased to exist with the fall of Jerusalem. We do not even know for certain that a legally constituted Sanhedrin existed at this time. Contemporary sources other than the Gospels mention only a sort of council of supporters of the king or the high priest, summoned especially on occasion to give moral backing to a decision; this was very different from the Great Sanhedrin that became the decisive body in Judaism after the fall of Jerusalem.

Peter's Treachery

PETER'S DENIAL OF Jesus was the ultimate assertion that Christ's kingship does not rely on human strength. Faced with a mere slip of a girl (this is the sense of the Greek word), the leader of the disciples denies his master, and then twice more, with increasing emphasis, repeats his treachery. By unpicking Mark's pitiless interweaving of Peter's denial with Jesus' steadfastness, Luke is gentler toward Peter, for the contrast is less strongly painted. It also makes a smoother transition from the meeting of the elders to the decision to hand Jesus over, if the denial does not intervene between them. For Luke, in any case, the point of the event is Peter's conversion. Luke increases the pathos of the scene by having Jesus himself nearby, near enough to be in eye contact. Only when Peter has shown his own complete emptiness does Jesus turn to him with a glance that brings about his own conversion, so that he may "strengthen his brothers," as Jesus prophesied at the supper. Luke also adds a touch to Peter's sorrow: "He wept *bitterly.*" The contrast with Judas is complete.

The Mockery of the Prophet

IN LUKE, THE maltreatment of Jesus is specifically mockery, with the physical abuse taking second place. It also changes the sense that the mockers are not the presumed dignified members of the Sanhedrin, but are those who were guarding Jesus. Jesus has been presented as a prophet throughout the Gospel, and now, ironically, his captors use this aspect to mock him. Their sadistic game is given more content, in that they not merely challenge him to prophesy, but, having blindfolded him, they challenge him to identify his strikers. As a prophet, neither the blindfold nor his ignorance of them should be a bar to his recognizing them. It is especially ironic that they are blind to the fact that his prophecy of Peter's denial has even now just been fulfilled.

JESUS BEFORE THE ELDERS

THIS INTERROGATION BEFORE the elders has a changed character in Luke from the Jewish hearing in Mark. There is no mention of the high priest, nor of Jesus' prophecy about the temple. This is, of course, because Luke's whole attitude to Jesus in the temple is different from that of Mark. The temple has played an important part in the Gospel right from the infancy stories onward, and will play an important part in the Jerusalem community in the early part of Acts. The temple is the center of Jesus' royal and messianic activity of teaching, just as it will be the center of the early Christian community in Jerusalem, and the center to which Paul constantly returns. Far from sweeping the temple away, Jesus has used it as his center for daily teaching.

Furthermore, the scene cannot any longer be called a "trial." There is no evidence, no verdict, and indeed when they bring Jesus before Pilate, they merely accuse him as though this scene had never occurred. At this Jewish interrogation Jesus is in control; the leaderless group of "elders of the people, chief priests and scribes" is no more than a foil to Jesus, enabling him to make two separate confessions or claims, that he is the Christ and that he is the Son of God. Whereas in Mark and Matthew Jesus is silent, in Luke he testifies on his own behalf, so that his own witness gives his opponents their impetus and they stress, "Why do we need any evidence? We have heard it for ourselves from his own lips" (22:71).

Jesus the Christ

EACH ACCUSATION NOW receives a new prominence. First of all, the authorities no longer merely ask Jesus whether he is the Christ, they demand that he proclaim it: "If you are the Christ, tell us!" Then Luke points out the futility of any attempt to convince the authorities: "If I tell you, you will not believe, and if I question you, you will not answer"—a resignation reminiscent of Abraham's rejection of the rich man's plea in the parable: "If they will not listen either to Moses or to the prophets, they will not be convinced even if someone should rise from the dead" (16:31). As in the Pilate scene, the stress will be upon the Jewish determination to have Jesus executed, so here it is on the stubbornness of Jesus' interrogators, and their refusal to accept the truth.

Furthermore, Luke significantly alters Jesus' own interpretation of "Christ." To the Marcan claim—immediately denounced by the high priest as blasphemy—that they will see the Son of Man sharing the awesome chariot throne of God, Luke makes two changes. It is no longer a matter of sight and in the future. It is a matter of fact and vividly present: not "you *will see*," but "from now on the Son of Man *will be seated* . . ." But significantly, although it is a matter of fact, his interrogators will not see it—presumably through this same stubbornness. Secondly, there is no "coming with the clouds of heaven." The interest is no longer in the second coming or the final judgment. As the second coming has continued to delay, Luke's interest has moved from the future to the present. The emphasis is not on the future coming but on the present exaltation of Christ. The Passion and resurrection are already the moment of the declaration of God's kingship.

So in this scene the Son of Man is presented as entering his glory now, and ready at the right hand of God to receive his faithful, just as he will be ready to welcome the first martyr, Stephen, who sees "the heaven thrown open and the Son of Man standing at the right hand of God" (Acts 7:56). Throughout the Passion narrative Luke is aware that Jesus in his Passion supports his followers in theirs.

Jesus the Son of God

THE SECOND QUESTION centers on the title "Son of God." This title is no longer joined to that of Christ, but receives a separate value of its own, in accordance with Luke's more developed understanding of the Lordship of Christ. Similarly at the annunciation the child is separately predicted as Christ and as Son of God. What is most significant is that all Jesus' opponents confess this dignity of Jesus: "They *all* said, 'So you are the Son of God, then?' He answered, 'It is you who say I am.' " The whole scene is more a declaration of Jesus' triumph than a humiliating trial.

REFLECTION
From now on the Son of Man will be seated at the right hand of God.

177

JESUS BEFORE PILATE

LUKE IS ALWAYS a careful historian. He has noted that Mark gives us no details of any charge preferred against Jesus before Pilate; Pilate just somehow seems to know that Jesus claims to be King of the Jews. Luke shows Jesus' captors giving definite charges. They are, of course, false; but some charges are required, and these are the sort of charges that could have been brought against Jesus on this occasion: subverting the people, preventing the payment of tribute to Caesar, and claiming to be Christ, a king. Luke is always keen to align the persecution of Jesus with that of his followers, to stress that he stands beside his followers in their trials. The charges against Jesus are described in terms similar to the charges preferred against Paul at Thessalonica: turning the whole world upside down, breaking Caesar's edicts, claiming that there is another king, Jesus (Acts 17:6–7). So in his trial before the Roman governor Jesus prefigures his follower Paul in his trial before the Roman magistrates.

Luke is also considerably more cautious than Mark about the Barabbas incident. There is no mention in Luke of any amnesty or regular custom of releasing a prisoner—a Marcan detail (Mark 15:6) which is not attested in external history, though there would be a certain appropriateness in the custom of releasing a prisoner at the festival of the release of the Israelites from captivity in Egypt. According to Luke, the crowd (or is it the leaders?) simply roar for the release of Barabbas, and are not to be put off by the offer of the release of Jesus. The contrast is all the stronger between Jesus, unjustly accused of subversion, and Barabbas, who had in fact been involved in a riot.

The Innocent Victim

LUKE'S CHIEF EMPHASIS is, however, on Pilate's recognition of the innocence of Jesus. Three times Pilate declares that he can find no case against this man, and three times the Jewish authorities react by insisting on pressing their case. With each declaration of Jesus' innocence, Pilate embraces a wider circle, first the charge that has been made, then any charge, and finally any evil at all.

It is only in Luke that Pilate first (v. 16) suggests that he whip Jesus (a lighter punishment than the vicious flogging of Mark and Matthew), and then actually wants to release him (v. 20). Finally Luke again stresses the responsibility of the Jewish leaders: Pilate "handed Jesus over to them to deal with as they pleased" (v. 25). The execution is not Pilate's will. He pronounces no sentence; indeed, it is even as though the Jews rather than the Romans actually carried out the execution. This emphatic insistence that the Roman authorities could find no case against Jesus is probably to be seen in the light of the later history of the Church: Luke wishes to show that in Roman eyes, Christianity is harmless and deserves no persecution.

Pontius Pilate

PILATE WAS GOVERNOR of Judea for ten years (A.D. 26–36). He is represented by the Jewish historian Josephus and the Jewish philosopher Philo as an unfeeling tyrant. But those authors are setting out to blacken Pilate's name in order to explain why the peaceable Jews were forced into rebellion a few years later against the Romans. Reading between the lines of Josephus' description of his period of office, it is possible to see that Pilate was well-meaning enough. For instance, he constructed an aqueduct to bring much-needed water into Jerusalem, and then found himself confronted by a riot when he tried to get the Jerusalem authorities to pay for it. When he mercifully quelled the riot with batons rather than swords, they claimed to be insulted. The Jews simply ran rings around him, and made any helpful initiative on his part look like a deliberate insult aimed against Jewish susceptibilities. Caiaphas was a wily operator, and was high priest for eighteen years, a most unusually long period to retain the office; he would know exactly how to twist Pilate's tail. It is easy to understand how Pilate first tried to avoid the responsibility of having Jesus executed and then capitulated into allowing an unjust execution by which the Jews seemed to set such store. Pilate's weakness is reflected in his final pathetic question, "What harm has he done?"

PRAYER
Lord, help me to be fair and just in my dealings with all people, and not to be swayed into injustice by human respect or fear of the powerful.

JESUS BEFORE HEROD

JESUS HAD FORETOLD that his followers would be taken for trial before governors and kings, and indeed this happens to Paul, when he is tried before the governors Festus and Felix and the king Agrippa II. The incident of Jesus before Herod shows that Jesus himself leads the way for his followers in being tried before governors and kings. In fact, Herod Antipas, tetrarch of Galilee and Perea, was not exactly a king. His father and several others of the Herod family were given the title of king, but he remained only a tetrarch, a negligible difference.

In the other Synoptic Gospels this Herod, son of King Herod the Great, has already appeared at his own birthday party as the murderer of John the Baptist. Luke omits this incident (the Baptist is quietly shuffled offstage even before Jesus' baptism, 3:19–20). The present encounter has, typically, been prepared by Luke with his mention that Herod was eager to see Jesus in 9:9.

The Herod incident occurs only in Luke. It takes the place of the mockery by the Roman soldiers. Historically, the referral of Jesus to the ruler of Galilee is not, however, improbable: As an ostentatiously pious Jew, Herod might well have made the pilgrimage to Jerusalem for the feast. His family had a magnificent palace in Jerusalem. At this time, according to Roman law, a prisoner could be judged in the *forum delicti* or the *forum domicilii*, that is, either where the supposed crime had been committed or where his domicile was—in the case of Jesus, this was Galilee. If Pilate wished to be rid of the case, it would have been a neat ploy to refer the prisoner to Herod. This he does as soon as he hears that Jesus' activity has been in Galilee.

Luke's Portrait of Herod

IT IS HARD to resist the impression that Herod, with typical Lucan vivacity, is represented as a rather wacky character. His reaction to having Jesus sent to him is excessive: The Greek, literally "he was too overjoyed"

(23:8), almost suggests whoops of joy. The same slightly maniacal overtone is given by the expression used for the interrogation, "at some length"; there is a hint of excess here. Then, frustrated at Jesus' silence, Herod literally "makes nothing of him" and descends to the indignity of joining his soldiery in this play-acting mockery. The "glittering" cloak in which Jesus was clothed was no doubt drawn from Herod's own wardrobe to add realism to the mockery of Jesus as a king. The same hysterical bonhomie is suggested by the reconciliation this made with Pilate (23:12). Such a reconciliation too is realistic: Herod Antipas acted as an agent for the emperor, keeping him informed of the activities of Roman officials in the area. This was notorious enough for Jesus to call him "that fox" (13:32). No one likes someone who reports behind his back to a superior, so it may well be that the cooperation between the two of them healed a breach. The reconciliation also, of course, serves the purpose of showing that even now Jesus brings peace and reconciliation wherever he goes, just as in his healing of the severed ear in Gethsemane.

The Silence of the Suffering Servant

THE SILENCE OF Jesus to Herod's questioning is a strong rebuke to Herod's intentions. Did Jesus reckon that Herod had not sufficient good-will to deserve an answer, since he would take no notice in any case, like the brothers of the rich man in the parable and the Jewish elders who interrogated him? The motif of Jesus silent before his persecutors occurs also in Mark's trial narrative, both before the Sanhedrin (Mark 14:61) and Pilate (15:4–5). Luke has transferred it to the interrogation by Herod. In this silence the Gospel writers see a fulfillment of the prophecy of the Suffering Servant of the Lord, "like a sheep dumb before its shearers." This prophecy of the Servant of the Lord, whose atoning death leads to his vindication by God and the glory of God, is a theme that runs through the Passion narrative.

REFLECTION

While the Jews demand miracles and the Greeks look for wisdom,
we are preaching a crucified Christ: to the Jews an obstacle they cannot
get over, to the Gentiles foolishness, but to those who have been called,
whether they are Jews or Greeks, a Christ who is both the power
of God and the wisdom of God. (1 Corinthians: 1:22–24)

THE WAY TO CALVARY

THE FINAL SCENES of Jesus' life interweave loyalty and disloyalty, cruelty and sorrow, crime and forgiveness. In this journey to execution, all the responsibility falls on the Jews. Crucifixion was a Roman punishment, and must have been carried out by the Romans rather than the Jews. Nevertheless, Luke, more strongly than Mark or Matthew, represents the Jewish authorities as responsible. At the end of the judgment scene, Pilate "handed Jesus over to them to deal with as they pleased." Now, immediately afterward, the phrase "as they were leading him away," must refer to the Jews and leave them in charge at least of the grim procession to execution. Luke is using the same words as Mark used to refer to the Roman soldiers who had been mocking Jesus, but his omission of that mockery changes the subject from the Roman soldiers to the Jewish leaders who had been demanding the death penalty.

Loyal Disciples

THIS HOSTILITY IS set against two scenes of loyalty. The first is the discipleship of Simon of Cyrene. Cyrene was an important trading port on the northern coast of Africa which—like many trading cities around the Mediterranean world—had an important Jewish population, important enough to be mentioned in several imperial decrees that have come down to us. Jews from Cyrene were present also among the many nations listed at Pentecost. Presumably there they had come up on pilgrimage for the feast, while here the note "coming in from the country" suggests (but no more) that Simon was now a farmer near Jerusalem. One might guess that his devotion to Jerusalem and to the promises of God brought him to move to Jerusalem.

Luke emphasizes the significance of carrying the cross. He has underlined the importance of the Christian carrying the cross *daily* (9:23), and that "no one can be my disciple without carrying the cross and coming after me" (14:27). Now, with two little touches he shows Simon as a model of such discipleship. He carries the cross specifically *"behind* Jesus." The tense of the verb used in Greek also indicates that it was not a momentary taking of the cross, but a long-term, lasting situation. Simon was taking on discipleship.

Discipleship is also the relationship implied by the next note, that large numbers of people *followed* him, for the word has regularly been used as the following that is discipleship. The groups mentioned have often been numbered among Jesus' supporters. The *people* have frequently stood in opposition to the leaders as enthusiastically supporting Jesus while the leaders cavil at him, and Luke has made a point of noting the support of the women who followed Jesus and his disciples.

The Final Lament

ON HIS WAY to Calvary, Jesus pronounces the last and most tragic of the laments for Jerusalem, so that his ministry in Jerusalem is bracketed at beginning and end by his sorrow at their failure to receive the message of peace. It had been prepared by Jesus' sadness as he approached Jerusalem on the great journey (13:34–35). Then the opening bracket of his ministry in Jerusalem was given as Jesus entered the city in 19:41–44. Now, as he leaves Jerusalem, comes the most solemn of all. It is so full of prophetic allusions and overtones that we are given clearly to understand that Jesus, the last of the prophets, is announcing the fulfillment of the dooms pronounced by so many of the Old Testament prophets against Jerusalem—with the solemn eschatological prophetic phrase, "the days are coming when . . ." "Daughters of Jerusalem" (or "Zion") was a phrase often used in reproach at the failure of Jerusalem to repent (Isaiah 3:16; 16:1), and in invitations to join in mourning for the devastation of Jerusalem. The blessing on those whose wombs are barren is a dreadful reversal of so much that has been positive in Jewish tradition about the family and the blessing of children, and in particular in Luke about the blessedness of the womb that bore Jesus and the breasts that he sucked. Even worse is the despairing cry, calling the hills and the mountains to hide them from the awesome wrath of God.

PRAYER

You have called me, Lord. I have no alternative to the choice of following you faithfully or refusing the call, as Jerusalem refused it. Grant me to respond and to follow your way of peace.

THE CRUCIFIXION

THERE WAS NO need to go into detail about the grisly process of fixing to the cross. They were all too familiar to the original readers of the Gospels. The spirituality of some ages has found it inspiring to dwell on the physical sufferings of Jesus. Others have found this a morbid distraction. As already pointed out, the early centuries of Christianity represented the triumph of Christ on the cross by a bejeweled cross rather than any realistic figure.

The Explanation from Scripture

THE MOST OBVIOUS feature of the explanation of the shame of the cross was that Jesus was obeying the will of his Father manifested in scripture. This is expressed by the density of scriptural quotations and allusions throughout the Passion narrative, but especially in the account of the crucifixion. The division of Jesus' clothing, the jeering of the leaders, the friends standing at a distance, Jesus' final prayer—all are described in terms that recall passages in scripture. To the modern mind, such detailed comparison, the product of the first-century Jewish approach to scripture, may fail to convey the meaning intended, and seem merely a series of fussily engineered coincidences. It is, however, the means of showing, by the exegetical methods of the time, that the scriptures and all the promises were fulfilled in the death of Jesus. Paul draws the threads together in his letter to the Romans, when he writes of the obedience of Christ, the second Adam, undoing the disobedience of the first Adam.

The Obedience of Jesus

HOW, IN PRACTICAL terms, was Jesus' acceptance of his death an act of obedience to his Father? Throughout the Gospel story, we have seen Jesus as the final prophet, proclaiming and manifesting the kingship of God by his miracles, teaching, authority, forgiveness. He chose a nucleus of disciples whom he formed to follow him. The climax of his teaching was the daily teaching in the temple, at the very center of the holy city of Jerusalem, God's dwelling on earth. Luke conveys vividly the ardor of his longing to make Jerusalem the center from which his teaching would spread. Luke shows us that the people (the People of God) responded, but the leaders persisted in their blindness, which caused him so much distress. His obedience was to accept the failure and rejection, not to divert or wilt away from his message at what he knew lay before him. On the merely human level, let alone as a prophet, he would have known that the leaders would not accept this challenge to their authority. Luke stresses his obedience through the noble calm with which he accepts his destiny. From the "agony" in Gethsemane to the willing resignation of his life into God's hands, Jesus is in charge of his destiny and voluntarily accepting it.

Golgotha

THE NAME MEANS "skull." Crucifixion was normally beside a road for maximum publicity, and all the Gospels record that the normal *titulus* was affixed to the cross, detailing the alleged crime for which the criminal was being executed. Not only would this increase the shame and agony of the victim; it would also act as a deterrent to others who saw the twisted result of such pretensions. The traditional place, venerated today as Calvary, is just outside the walled city as it then was, beside the road to Joppa (Jaffa) on the coast. There was clearly a slight hill there into the rock of which tomb chambers have been dug. Presumably the place of crucifixion got its name as a knoll of rock in the shape of a skull. Since that time (possibly under the emperor Hadrian) this hill has been quarried away for building stone, leaving only a "sugar lump" of rock, some thirty feet cubed. This cube seems to have been left because it is flawed by a great vertical cleft down the middle, which makes it useless for building. Pious legend attributes this cleft to the earthquake at the death of Jesus.

Prayer

Lord Jesus, you were obedient in all things to the will of your Father. Grant me the courage to follow your example. When the way is hard and painful, let me remember your steadfast and unflinching obedience, and obey with the same loving devotion which you showed.

THE CRUCIFIED JESUS

THE FIRST PART of verse 34, "Father, forgive them; they do not know what they are doing," is absent in some good manuscripts. Some scholars think these words are original and were cut out by some very early editor in an anti-Semitic attempt to obliterate the forgiveness of the Jews (though the executioners were surely Roman). Others think that they form an original saying of Jesus, inserted here later in part of the manuscript tradition. In any case, they form an invaluable glimpse of Jesus practicing the forgiveness he taught others, for instance in the Lord's Prayer, and continue to illustrate the divine forgiveness that has featured so importantly in Luke's Gospel. When Stephen is being stoned to death, he, too, makes a similar prayer for his executioners, but addressed to Jesus, "Lord, do not hold this sin against them." Here again we see the disciple imitating his master in suffering, and so carrying on the life of Jesus in the Christian community.

It is also a lovely prayer, beginning, "Father," so that Jesus' first words and his last words on Calvary testify to his affection for his Father, and his obedience to him. In Semitic thought such a "bracketing" process qualifies everything between the brackets, so that Jesus' state of mind on Calvary is being characterized as continuously in loving union with the Father.

The Mockers

LUKE MAKES A sharp distinction between the people and their leaders. The people merely look on; we shall hear more of their frame of mind later. The leaders mock Jesus, chiding him with being a Messiah who saved others and cannot even save himself. The irony is exquisite, that at the very moment of the completion of his messiahship, when he is indeed saving others at such voluntary cost to himself, he should be reproached with inability to save. This is the central point of the mockery: Each of the mockers in turn challenges him to save, the leader, the soldiers, the thief.

The soldiers also join in to make fun of him. They offer him "vinegar" to quench his thirst. Perhaps the basis of this is offering him a drink of the cheap wine they would have for themselves. It could originally have been a gesture of kindness. But the "vinegar" is the fulfillment of a psalm verse describing the mockery of an innocent sufferer. Their mockery of him as "King of the Jews" (not in Mark or Matthew) is especially significant in view of the declaration of his kingship. This has been becoming clearer and clearer since, at Jericho, on the last stage of the journey to Jerusalem, Bartimaeus hailed him as "Son of David." Now the soldiers do not realize how right they are, and their irony brings the declaration of his kingship to a moment of climax.

The Two Thieves

IN MARK AND Matthew the two thieves are merely sketched. It is as though they are simply a fulfillment of the scriptural passage, quoted by Luke at the last supper: "He was counted as one of the rebellious" (22:37). Luke, however, characteristically gives them each a vivid character and a lively dialogue. Luke likes to balance men and women in his stories, and it has been suggested that in their contrast these two men are the male counterpart of the contrasting sisters Martha and Mary. The one thief joins in the taunts. More important, the "good thief" is the embodiment of repentance and discipleship. He admits not once but twice his own guilt: "We deserved it: We are paying for what we did." One might even suggest that perhaps his reasoning is a little too literary and philosophical for his situation, more adapted to Luke's cast of mind than to the circumstances! In Luke's story of the call of the disciples, Peter is not called to be a disciple until he has confessed that he is a sinner. Like Peter, once he has confessed his sinfulness, the good thief is promised the kingdom. Even to the last, Jesus is exercising his mission of reconciling the repentant. To the last, he is opening the kingdom to sinners.

PRAYER

Bring me, Lord, to repentance in the end. Make me never too proud to admit my faults. In my own trials let me feel my solidarity with yours, that you may take me to join you in your kingdom.

THE DEATH OF JESUS

WITHOUT INTRODUCING ANY new facts or events, Luke gives a different and quite special atmosphere to the death of Jesus. The first striking feature is the calm and peace. The horror has disappeared. In the other Synoptic Gospels the death of Jesus follows immediately on a general stir around the cross. There is the cry of Jesus, "My God, my God, why have you forsaken me?" which has been construed as a cry of despair; in fact, it is the opening of Psalm 22, a psalm describing the suffering and rejection of the Just Man, which leads on to his vindication and the glory of God, all of which must be presumed to be present in Jesus' mind. There is the incident of the soldier running for the sponge, and the mocking misunderstanding of the Hebrew words *eli, eli* ("My God, my God") as a summons to the prophet Elijah, a traditional figure of liberation from foreign oppression.

In Luke there is none of this. The final cry of Jesus in Mark is left unexplained. In Luke it is a prayer of confident trust, again beginning "Father," and at this dire moment confirming the loving relationship of Jesus with his Father. After he has declared that he is ready, Jesus breathes his last.

The word for "breath" and "spirit" is the same in Greek and Hebrew. It is tempting to see in the word used to describe the moment of Jesus' death (literally "he breathed out") a reference to the Holy Spirit, which will play such an important part in the future of Jesus' community. It is not so pointed as in John, when Jesus literally "*gave up* his spirit (or breath)" at his death. But the overtone may be there, that the moment of Jesus' death is the moment when the Spirit that was to inspire the community became available.

The Signs

THE SIGNIFICANCE OF the death of Jesus is highlighted by two phenomena, darkness over the earth and the rending of the temple veil. Originally these were perhaps to be understood symbolically, but by adding small details Luke makes sure that they are viewed as real historical events. The darkness at noon must originally be seen as a fulfillment of Amos' prophecy of the Day of the Lord, that terrible day of judgment, when "I shall make the sun go down at noon and darken the earth in broad daylight" (Amos 8:9). It indicated, then, that this day was the fulfillment and completion of God's plan. Luke turns the symbolic dimension into a rational, factual account by giving the explanation "the sun's light failed," as an eclipse of the sun. The other sign, the rending of the veil of the temple, is also understood in a physical sense, by the addition of the pictorial "was torn *right down the middle.*" It must originally have had the sense of a symbol of the end of Judaism. This coincides with a tradition mentioned by Josephus that an omen of the destruction of the temple in A.D. 70 was given by the veil that hung over the doorway being mysteriously torn from top to bottom forty years earlier (signifying an indefinite, long period of preparation, like the forty years in the desert). This dating would, of course, bring the incident near the date of the crucifixion.

The Reactions

BEFORE HIS DEATH, Jesus was mocked by three groups, the leaders of the Jews, the soldiers, and the thief. After his death, we hear of three groups of his supporters, the centurion who recognizes that he was "an upright man," the crowds, and the disciples. In Mark's Gospel the centurion was the first human being to acknowledge Jesus as "Son of God," and so mark the completion of the revelation of Jesus' personality. In Luke's version the use of "upright" is more in line with his sophisticated and philosophical bent.

The reaction of the crowds at the cross is the typical Lucan reaction of repentance and praise, a sense of unworthiness coupled with wonder and gratitude at the glory of God. So the series of conversions is complete, Peter brought back to strengthen his brethren after his failure, the daughters of Jerusalem, the good thief, and now the whole gathering of witnesses. These stand for those who will in the future be brought to repentance and conversion by the cross of Jesus. Present also are the two silent groups of disciples, men and women, watching at a distance, so fulfilling Psalm 38:11: "Friends and companions shun my disease, even the dearest of them *keep their distance.*"

PRAYER
Father, into your hands I commit my spirit.

189

THE BURIAL OF JESUS

THE IMPORTANCE OF the burial of Jesus for Luke is first, of course, the preparation for the accounts of the empty tomb and the resurrection, but second—and perhaps of more importance to Luke personally—that the Gospel story has come full circle.

Joseph of Arimathea

THE STORY BEGAN in Jerusalem with Zechariah, a priest and so a member of the Jewish establishment, who was, like Joseph of Arimathea, good and upright, observant of the Law in all its particulars. The next establishment figure we met, in the temple, was Simeon, who, again like Joseph, lived in the hope of seeing the kingdom of God. Luke has always been concerned with the salvation of Israel, how it is that the promises of God to Israel can have been fulfilled although Jesus was rejected. On the whole, his solution has been that part, at any rate, of the nation responded to Jesus. There is a sharp distinction between the leaders and the people; the latter accept Jesus eagerly, while the former acrimoniously reject him. Now, however, we see that even the leaders of the Jews were not uniformly hostile to Jesus. Joseph is from the heart of the establishment, from one of the cities of Judea and a member of the council, and yet a good and upright man who had had no part in the reprehensible dealings of the Sanhedrin.

In the slightly later legislation the burial of criminals was in the charge of a council department, the Lower Beth Din (or House of Judgment). Part of the penalty and disgrace of criminal execution was that the body might not be buried by relatives, but was to be placed in a municipal tomb for a year, until it had decayed. The relatives might then collect the bones. It has been suggested that Joseph was the member of this Lower Beth Din charged with this matter, by a happy accident a pious and open member of the council. Even though Joseph was an official, he must ask Pilate for the body. This is additional proof that, despite some appearances in Luke, the execution was a Roman affair, carried out by Romans and under the authority of the Roman governor.

Burial in Jerusalem

TO MAKE SENSE of the accounts, it is essential to understand funeral arrangements in Jerusalem. The ground is uniformly rocky. A traditional six-foot burial in the earth is out of the question. At the time of Jesus the normal tomb was an underground stone chamber, reached down a flight of steps. Leading off this stone chamber (perhaps some ten feet square) were half a dozen shafts big enough to receive a body. There the body was left till it had perished enough for the bones to be collected and placed in a sarcophagus, a sort of stone box. The accounts of Jesus' burial stress that this tomb was new and hitherto unused. This emphasis is partly out of respect for Jesus (many of the surviving used tombs are insanitary and unattractive), partly in preparation for the discovery of the empty tomb: There was no possibility of mistake over the vanished body.

The observance of correct burial ritual has always been regarded as an important part of respect for the dead. The matter of spices and ointments for burial has produced some confusion in the Gospels. In Mark, the women are bringing the spices on Easter morning when they find the empty tomb. The disgrace of Jesus being buried without due anointing has, however, already been avoided by the anointing "for burial" at Bethany two days before the Passover. Luke omits this scene, replacing some of its elements with the story of the sinful woman (7:36–50, no. 28). It is therefore all the more important that the body should be duly anointed, which does not seem to have been barred by its criminal status. However, due piety also demanded that they rest on the sabbath day, though there seems a little confusion about this. Luke says that the sabbath was already dawning, as though he thought that the sabbath began at dawn, when in fact it begins at sundown on Friday, which we would regard as the previous evening. The solution is perhaps that Luke adopted "beginning to grow light" from Matthew's account of the discovery of the empty tomb.

PRAYER

Lord, your day of rest between your gruesome death and your glorious resurrection is still precious, enabling us to assimilate that moment, and to see that you shared our mortal condition. Grant me to value the peace and special sanctity of that day.

THE EMPTY TOMB

THE CHRISTIAN FAITH is founded on the resurrection of Christ, and the experience of the risen Christ in the community. This is the content of the earliest proclamation as conveyed by Paul (e.g., 1 Corinthians 15:3–5). He writes that he *received* this from the Lord and *handed* it *on*—the technical terms of the rabbinic process of tradition. Paul does not mention the empty tomb. It has been suggested that the story of the empty tomb as we have it now, with its stress on time and place, was originally the kernel of a liturgy at the place where the tomb was venerated, just as the story of the institution of the eucharist was originally (and still is) the kernel of the eucharistic liturgy.

The emphasis in the story as told by Mark was on the wonder of the event, the awe and fear of the women at the explanation of the empty tomb given by the heavenly messenger. This terrified amazement springs from the fact that the resurrection of the dead, which was expected to occur at the end of time, has already now occurred. God has acted in history as he was to act on the last day, and the last time has therefore burst upon them. As so often, Luke's emphasis can best be seen by comparison with the way Mark tells his story.

All Luke's accounts of the resurrection appearances are in Jerusalem. Mark's angel of the tomb directs Peter and the other disciples to Galilee, where they are to see the risen Christ. In Matthew and John 21, there are corresponding appearances in Galilee. Not so in Luke. For him, Jerusalem is the pivot to which Jesus journeys for his final ministry and death, where the risen Christ is seen, and from which the kerygma spreads to the ends of the earth. Accordingly, the angelic message is subtly changed. Instead of "He is going ahead of you *to* Galilee; that is where you will see him, just as he told you" (Mark 16:7, referring to 14:28), the message is "Remember what he told you *when he was still in* Galilee" (24:6).

The Reality of the Risen Body

LUKE'S FIRST EMPHASIS is on the physical reality of the resurrection. Thus, he stresses that the tomb was really empty. In Mark, the women enter the tomb and first see the angel. They are invited to see "the place where they laid him" but there is no record that they actually did so, which would be necessary were it a proof text for the emptiness of the tomb. Luke, on the other hand, adds that "they could not find the body of the Lord Jesus." It may be also that the dual witness of the two angels is introduced for this purpose, since in Jewish law two witnesses are required for proof. In the same vein, in the story of the appearance to the disciples gathered in the upper room, the physical reality of the risen body of Jesus is shown by his actually eating a piece of grilled fish before their eyes (24:42). In the same way Luke had insisted at the baptism that the Spirit descended "in a physical form," and will insist at Pentecost that the Spirit descends in the form of tongues of fire.

The Proclamation of the Risen Christ

THE ANGELS GIVE the first glimpse of the proclamation which will echo through the stories of the appearances of the risen Christ and through the pages of the Acts of the Apostles: "The Son of Man was destined to be handed over into the power of sinful men and be crucified, and rise again on the third day." This is to be the basic form of the message that is at the center of all the speeches of Peter and Paul in their apostolate, from Jerusalem to Rome. The messengers underline three facets of this. It is all the fulfillment of the will of God expressed in scripture, since it "was destined" to happen. It is the fulfillment of what was prophesied during Jesus' ministry, since "they remembered his words." The diffusion of the message is under the authority of Jesus himself: "Remember what he told you."

The stage is almost set for the proclamation of the Acts. The risen Christ will himself twice give the example of the proclamation, to the disciples on the way to Emmaus, and to the Eleven assembled in the upper room. For their own opportunity to make the proclamation the disciples will have to wait for the advent of the Spirit at Pentecost.

PRAYER

Christ is now risen again, from his death and all his pain. Therefore will we merry be and rejoice with him always, alleluia.

THE MESSAGE TO
THE ELEVEN

~❦~

THE STORY OF the finding of the empty tomb occurs in all the Gospels, albeit with a range of variations. After that, however, comes a variety of stories testifying to the appearances of the risen Jesus experienced by various members of the community. The most primitive tradition recorded by Paul in 1 Corinthians (15:3–5) mentioned appearances to Cephas (that is, the Aramaic equivalent of "Peter"), the Twelve, five hundred of the brothers at the same time, James, then all the apostles. Apart from these, Matthew and John share a tradition about an appearance to Mary Magdalene (and other women) near the tomb, Luke and John at least one appearance to the Twelve in the upper room. Matthew and the appendix to John have widely differing traditions of an appearance in Galilee, a tradition at which Mark also hints.

There is also a strong tradition of skepticism. This may first of all lie behind the strange notice in Mark 16:8 that the women who went first to the tomb "ran away" and "said nothing to nobody, for they were afraid." As it stands in Greek (as translated above), this verse shows all the features of Mark's personal style (the emphasis on fear and amazement, a double negative, and the explanation added with "for") which occur frequently throughout his Gospel and serve as fingerprints of his own composition. But it certainly attests to the tradition of noncommunication of the message. Luke has the complete reverse, which nevertheless has the same effect. In Luke there is still noncommunication of the message, but for an entirely different reason: The women tell the Eleven, and they refuse to receive the message. To this is added the single verse about Peter's amazement and incomprehension.

The same need to be persuaded recurs in every story. In Matthew's story of the appearance on the mountain in Galilee some hang back from doing reverence. In John both Mary Magdalene and Peter fail at first to recognize the risen Christ. At the appearance in the upper room "doubting

Thomas" voices the hesitations with explosive vigor. The whole tradition, therefore, is concerned to show that belief in the resurrection was no pushover, but had to be impressed upon the frightened survivors of Jesus' band of followers.

Luke and the Women

THIS IS THE final instance in Luke where women come out ahead! Throughout the Gospel he has shown the sensitivity of women to the divine message, from the contrast between Zechariah and Mary onward. On the whole, there has been a consistent pairing of women with men: Simeon and Anna, the two children raised to life (the one a son with a mother, the other a daughter with a father), the widow and the traveler at midnight both examples for persistence in prayer, all Jesus' friends (male) *and* the women watching on Calvary. Repeatedly, also, the reader has been reminded of the faithful band of women who looked after Jesus. Above all, Luke has been careful to paint Mary as the model of discipleship, hearing the word of God and keeping it. Now it is the women who are open to the message of the resurrection, and the chosen men who refuse to accept it.

Peter at the Tomb

A SINGLE VERSE relates the story of Peter's puzzlement at the tomb. This is perhaps the strongest of all the traditions of failure to believe. (It is omitted in some versions because one stream of the manuscript tradition lacks this verse. But all the three great manuscripts have it.) The story comes again in John, and the same tradition must underlie both versions. In John the failure of Peter is expressed even more strongly. In John the "beloved disciple" is the expression of love and openness, the icon of the Christian disciple. He is added to this story as he was added to the story of Peter's denial during the Passion. His belief contrasts with Peter's disbelief. In Luke it is merely blank amazement, the seedbed of belief.

PRAYER

Lord, grant me an openness to your word, but also a firm skepticism. Give me a strong faith, but help me to avoid that credulity that reduces your saving truths to silliness and brings contempt upon your generosity.

THE ROAD TO EMMAUS

OF ALL LUKE'S brilliantly told stories this is perhaps the most memorable. From the literary point of view its symmetry is superb: It starts and ends in Jerusalem; within this frame the disciples converse at both beginning and end; within this, Jesus first appears and finally disappears; within this, their eyes are first held from recognizing him and then finally opened to recognize him. At the center stands the message of the resurrection and its explanation. The story is told with all Luke's feeling for character: First the disciples are walking along, morose and wrapped up in their own sorrows; then their disappointment explodes into sarcasm, which gradually gives way to warmth, an invitation to the stranger to remain with them, and finally hospitality and eucharistic participation as their confidence returns. The delicacy of the stranger as he gradually draws them out, and the allusiveness of the gesture whose significance they realize in time only to find that he has left them, are finely painted. Especially positive is the contrast between the sad and lonely walk at the start, and the joyful, thronging gathering at the end.

A Model of Church Life

THE STORY PROVIDES a model for life in the Christian community in two ways, both the sacraments and instruction. From the sacramental viewpoint there is a remarkable and deliberate parallel with the story in the Acts, of Philip and the Ethiopian. There also Luke gives the story of a journey, in which a seemingly chance comer and stranger explains the gospel message from the scriptures; there follows a sacrament (the eucharist in the case of the journey to Emmaus; in the case of the Ethiopian, baptism), and finally the stranger disappears. In both cases, therefore, we are given the model of scriptural instruction leading to sacramental participation in the life of Christ. In the case of the meal at Emmaus, it is precisely in the breaking of bread that Christ is recognized, acknowledged, and accepted.

In both these cases the model of scriptural instruction is the salient feature. The story functions as a sort of paradigm of the Christian apostolate. The angel at the empty tomb has already given a brief example of this process, but the Emmaus story is far more explicit. By a literary device of Lucan brilliance the travelers tell us again, and more fully, the story of the empty tomb and the reactions to it. Then the risen Christ explains the meaning of what has happened as the fulfillment of the prophecies. Moses and the prophets lead directly to their destined fulfillment in the Passion and the entry into glory which is its consequence. Without this, the events are inexplicable and make no sense. At the end of his Gospel, therefore, as in the Old Testament emphasis of the infancy narratives, Luke underlines that the Christ event is the completion of the promises to Israel.

The Prophet in Word and Deed

ONCE AGAIN, JESUS is presented—not by himself but by the disappointed disciples—as a prophet powerful in word and deed (the evidence of his authority throughout the Gospel). It is the task of a prophet not merely to foretell the future, but to interpret the present, to read it through God's eyes. This Jesus now proceeds to do by explaining the recent happenings in the light of the scripture. He is also the model for the Christian evangelist, whose task it will be to show why it was necessary that the Christ should enter into his glory only by passing through suffering and death.

The conclusion of the journey with the eucharist is also an important indication of the Christian life. That the meal is a eucharist is suggested by the use of the identical terms at this meal of Jesus with his disciples that were used both at the miraculous feeding in the desert and at the last supper. At the latter he had charged the disciples to repeat the action in his memory. Now he himself does so, and thereby creates his community, for in this moment the eyes of the disciples are opened, they reach understanding of what has happened, and they enter into community with him. The eucharist is the meeting of the community with the risen Lord, which in itself both brings to faith and creates the community.

PRAYER

When all seems dark and disappointing, Lord, bring me your company.
If I turn to you and see your way from suffering to glory, you will open
my eyes and make me part of your company.

JESUS APPEARS TO
THE ELEVEN

THE FINAL SCENE of the Gospel appears to take place still on the Sunday of the resurrection, though it hardly fits that the two disciples should have rushed back the seven miles from Emmaus after the evening meal (steeply uphill!) in time for the final blessing on the outskirts of Bethany. The dramatic unity is more important than the details.

It shows the inner group of the disciples being prepared for their mission. The appearance of the risen Christ provokes the reaction of awed disbelief which is a feature of all the resurrection appearances. One particular Lucan feature is that they are prevented from recognizing him by their joy at seeing him; Luke is perhaps the most joyful of the Gospels— from the first moment of Jesus' birth rejoicing and singing on earth and in heaven are keynotes. The risen Jesus explains and shows that his body is real: He is not a ghost. He has hands and feet (there is no mention of nail scars either here or in the crucifixion account of Luke) and he eats a piece of fish before their eyes. Yet always the disciples have difficulty in recognizing him. Awe and fear is only one component in this. The resurrection was not a mere resuscitation, as the miraculous raisings from the dead in the course of the Gospel story (Jairus' daughter, the boy from Nain, Lazarus) seem to have been. It involved transposition into the glorious sphere of God, and this somehow must have had an effect on his appearance.

The Risen Body

WE CAN PERHAPS form some cloudy idea of how different the appearance of the risen Christ was, by appeal to Paul. When in 1 Corinthians 15 Paul is teaching about how the risen body will be, he uses the image of the seed, which dies in the ground before fructifying. The transformation is described by Paul in terms of four changes, or three summed up in a fourth. Each is a transference into the sphere and power of God: "What is sown is perishable, but what is raised is imperishable" (all potential for decay is removed); "What is sown is contemptible, but what is raised is glorious" (there is no possibility of failure, but all is suffused with the awesome divine glory); "What is sown is weak, but what is raised is powerful" (with God's own limitless power); "what is sown is a natural body, and what is raised is a spiritual body" (the inner dynamism of the body is no longer the soul, but then is the Spirit of God). Such a change could well be somehow visible in the physical appearance of the same person, so that his friends would be awestruck from recognizing him.

The Commission

THE SCENE IS closely allied to the account of Christ's appearance in the upper room on the evening of the day of resurrection in John. The chief difference is that Jesus does not now breathe on them his Spirit, for in Luke the Spirit is merely promised now, and its imparting is reserved till Pentecost. There is the same greeting, "Peace be with you," and as we have seen, for Luke the gospel is above all a message of peace. Peace was the greeting of the angels at Jesus' birth, and the way of peace in the message of Jesus was what Jerusalem failed to recognize.

The final instructions of the risen Christ to his disciples again, as in all the resurrection appearances in Luke, stress that the key to understanding what has happened lies in the scripture. The angels at the empty tomb had already explained the event by reference to the scripture, and the stranger on the way to Emmaus explained the happenings in Jerusalem in relation to the prophets from Moses onward. "It was written:" Scripture and all the prophecies have been fulfilled in the death and resurrection of Jesus.

The other keynote is that they are to preach repentance. Luke has consistently underlined the need for repentance, and the welcome to sinners given by Jesus and his Father. Repentance will be the final appeal of all the great missionary speeches in Acts, as the apostles carry out this commission. A change of heart is necessary for every approach to Jesus.

PRAYER

Lord, grant me to recognize you as you come to me in the word of your Church, and give me the change of heart to embrace your way of peace.

THE ASCENSION

The Timing

LUKE IS THE only Gospel writer to mention the ascension, and he describes it twice, once here and once at the beginning of Acts. There is a puzzle about the timing of the event. In the Gospel it seems to occur on the day of the resurrection itself, though the time indication is vague ("then"), and it makes a very full day. In the Acts it occurs only after forty days—and these are both by the same author, who is acutely aware that his composition is to be read as a single work in two parallel volumes. It clearly simply was not a problem to him, just as in the Acts he can tell the story of Paul's conversion three times, each time with minor and incompatible variations. The Jewish historian Josephus often tells the story of the same event differently in his two major volumes, *Antiquities of the Jews* and *Jewish War*.

Forty days in biblical language means a fairly long, indefinite period, often a period of preparation. Israel is forty years in the desert, preparing to enter the promised land. Elijah remains forty days in the desert of Horeb, preparing for his mission of preaching, and Jesus himself remains forty days in the desert, being tested before he begins to proclaim the kingdom. It is therefore eminently fitting that his disciples should be prepared for their mission by Jesus' final instructions over a period of forty days.

The Blessing

THE FINAL ACTION of Jesus is a solemn priestly blessing. "Raising his hands" indicates just such a priestly gesture, but is full of priestly reminiscences. It is used, of course, of Moses raising his hands to insure victory for the Israelites against the Amalekites. Overtones must be especially present from the blessing of Aaron in Leviticus 9:22, for this is the conclusion of the investiture of the priests, and its immediate realization is in the manifestation of the power of the Lord as "a flame leapt out from

Yahweh's presence." Just so, the preparation of the disciples for their mission can be seen as a priestly investiture, concluded by the coming of the Spirit at Pentecost in the form of tongues of fire.

"He Was Taken Up into Heaven"

TO THE MODERN mind, this picture raises difficulties about a three-decker universe, the Hebrew conception of a three-layered creation, heaven above, the earth, and the underworld beneath. We are too familiar with paintings of a pair of feet still protruding from a cloud, and with the question, "Where is his body now?" The cloud is in fact the symbol of the divinity. The cloud over the tent of meeting or in the temple is always the sign of the presence of God, so that when (in the account in Acts) the cloud takes Jesus from their sight, this is a statement of his being taken up into the Godhead. The immediately following incident of the coming of the Spirit at Pentecost shows that he is being withdrawn merely in order to return in a more powerful mode of presence.

There is a further dimension of the scene that concludes the presentation of Jesus which has been so important in Luke. Throughout the Gospel we have seen that Jesus is a prophet in the line of the Old Testament prophets. He is the climax of the messengers sent by God to his people, and as a prophet brings God's promises to a conclusion. The two great prophets of the tradition, Moses and Elijah, were both said to be taken up into heaven at the end of their lives. Now becomes obvious another dimension of the narrative of the transfiguration, when Moses and Elijah were seen speaking to Jesus about his passing (literally "exodus") which he was to accomplish at Jerusalem (9:31). The most similar to the ascension is the departure of Elijah in a chariot of fire. It is also the most significant, for as Elijah departs, his spirit descends upon his successor, Elisha, who then, clothed with this spirit, continues his mission. So the conclusion of the Gospel is at the same time a preparation for the further mission which will be chronicled in the Acts of the Apostles.

PRAYER
Lord, grant me your Spirit, that I may continue your mission.
Let me be your presence in the world, guided by your Spirit and faithful
to your ways in all I do.

NOTES